TALES OF

SWORDFISH AND TUNA

WORLD'S RECORD BROADBILL SWORDFISH TO DATE 1926. CAUGHT AT AVALON, JUNE 29, 1926. 582 POUNDS

PLATE I

Tales of
SWORDFISH
and
TUNA

by
ZANE GREY

THE DERRYDALE PRESS
LANHAM AND NEW YORK

THE DERRYDALE PRESS

Published in the United States of America
by The Derrydale Press
4720 Boston Way, Lanham, Maryland 20706

Distributed by NATIONAL BOOK NETWORK, INC.

Original Derrydale printing 1991
First paperback with french folds 2000

Library of Congress Cataloging-in-Publication Data

Grey, Zane, 1872-1939.
  Tales of the swordfish and tuna / by Zane Grey.
      p.   cm.
  Originally published : New York : Harper & Brothers, 1927.
    ISBN 1-58667-027-1 (pbk. : alk. paper)
    1. Swordfish fishing. 2. Tuna fishing. I. Title.

SH671.S8 G7 2000
799.1'778—dc21   00-035837

TO MY BROTHER R. C.

In memory of the old Zanesville boyhood days that made us fishermen. In memory of your first fishing experience when you were six years old, red-headed, freckle-faced and barefooted. In memory of the years with their poignant trials of life, their defeats and victories, and the lesson of the murmuring brooks, the swift rivers and the vast mysterious sea—that lesson of romance and joy in nature, and the reward of courage and endurance.

ZANE GREY

CONTENTS

ILLUSTRATIONS

ILLUSTRATIONS

TALES OF

SWORDFISH AND TUNA

WORLD'S RECORD BLUE-FIN TUNA TO DATE 1926. CAUGHT IN NOVA SCO-
TIA, AUGUST 22, 1924. 758 POUNDS

PLATE II

I

TUNA AT AVALON, 1919

THE 1919 season for tuna at Avalon was the best for many years. What it might have been if the round-haul net-boats had not haunted the channel, taking thousands of tons of tuna, no one could conjecture. Tuna were never before seen there in such numbers, both large and small.

But no matter how wonderful the fishing, it was spoiled by the Austrian and Jap net-boats. These round-haul boats have nets half a mile long and several hundred feet deep. When they surround a school of tuna it is seldom that any escape. If the tuna are very large, over one hundred pounds, then a great many of them are destroyed. Sometimes the weight of a large school is so great that the netters cannot handle it. In which case they take on board all they can dispose of and let the rest sink. Some of the tons of tuna go to the canneries at San Pedro, and a good many of them go to the fertilizer plants. These market fishermen are aliens, and they break the state and federal laws every day during the season. Catalina Island has a three-mile limit, inside of which no net-boat is permitted to haul. One day this season I counted sixteen round-haul net-boats within half a mile of Avalon Bay, and some of them were loaded so heavily that they sank in the water nearly to their gunwales, and the others were hauling their nets as fast as power and muscle could do it. I counted twenty Austrians pulling on one net. It was so full of tuna that they could scarcely budge it.

No wonder I was sick with anger and disgust and bade the tuna good-by.

During the season I caught a good many tuna, more, in fact, than ever before. Captain Danielson averred that it was the best season I ever had at Catalina. This was owing to my catches of blue-button tuna. The Tuna Club of Avalon recognizes only fish that weigh over one hundred pounds. I may say that it took me five years to catch my first blue-button fish. In 1919 my big tuna weighed 117 pounds, 114, 111, 109, and 109. My brother R. C. caught one of 107 pounds. Apparently this looks like remarkably good luck. But when I think of all the bad luck I had, the good seems small in proportion.

I have no idea how many very large tuna I hooked and lost on twenty-four-thread lines during July and August. But there must have been at least twenty-five. I had exceptionally good fortune in locating schools of large tuna. Captain Dan and I were always roaming the sea, peering for the white spouts of water on the horizon.

One day when we had guests aboard and they were fishing, I put out a bait on my light tackle and trolled it close behind the boat. Immediately there came a splash and a heavy pull. I had hooked a big tuna on my light outfit. The others, of course, had to reel in. My fish

R. C. Grey with 149-pound Pacific Tuna

PLATE III

Six Blue-Fin Tuna Caught at Avalon in One Day.   Average 118 Pounds

PLATE IV

made the long fast diving run that is usually so destructive to tackle. But he stopped short of two hundred
yards, and so for the moment I saved him. Captain Dan
buckled a belt on me, and I stood up, with the rod in the
belt socket, and began to work on that fish. Work meant
to pull and lift all the rod would stand, then lower it
quickly and wind the reel. It is fun for only a little
while! My ambition, of course, was to land a hundred-
pound tuna on light tackle—something which had not
yet been done. So I was in deadly earnest. So was
Captain Dan. This fish was so loggy and rolly that we
decided he was a yellow-fin tuna of very large size.
There are two kinds of tuna, yellow-fin and blue-fin.

My brother and our guests made considerable fun of
me as I heroically struggled with that tuna. I would lift
him and wind him up a hundred feet or so, and then he
would take the line away from me. It happened so often
that it must have looked funny. All of a sudden my tuna
started to sound. He did not run. He just plugged
down and down and down. The reel screamed zee—
zee—zee! This procedure grew alarming. Two hundred yards—three hundred yards—three-fifty, and
finally four hundred yards of line he took straight down.
This was the deepest I ever had any fish sound up to that
date. Captain Dan stood beside me, watching the reel.
He shook his head at every zee. My rod lay in the hollow
of my left elbow and the tip was doubled straight down.
The zee—zee—zee grew markedly shorter in time and
farther apart. Tremendous pressure of water on that
tuna had begun to tell. Most remarkable about this
incident was the fact that the nine-thread line had not
broken. It resembled a very tight, wet banjo string.
Finally the tuna stopped. I had half an inch of thick-
ness of line left on the reel-spool. Then I began to work,
carefully lifting and winding. Inch by inch! And after

a while foot by foot! This was harder work than heavy tackle. It took an hour to pump that tuna back up to his original position. I was as wet as if I had fallen overboard.

For two more hours I heaved and wound, gaining and losing in about the same proportion. What spurred me on was a certainty that little by little the tuna was weakening. But it was so little! The others on board stopped making game of me. They began to realize that this was a fight seldom recorded in the annals of angling. Besides, I must have been an object to excite wonder and pity, perhaps awe. My tuna hung around near the boat, sometimes rising toward the surface, to one side or the other, but mostly straight down. That is what makes a tuna fight so laborsome.

The very thing I feared he began again. He started down. Zee—zee—zee! Slower this time. Captain Dan left the wheel and stood beside me, watching the reel. I laid the rod over my left arm, and watched, too. Zee—zee—zee! It was terrible to see all that hard-earned line slip off and off and off. I would lose him this time. That was inevitable. Zee—zee—zee! He plugged down. I could feel him banging the leader with his tail. Slower and slower the line paid off. It seemed ages in going. I began to see red. I wanted him to hurry and break off. But more than that I hoped desperately that he would stop. How short and slow and squeaky the zees! At last he got out as much line as he had taken on the first occasion. There were four hundred and fifty yards on the reel. Captain Dan threw up his big hands and groaned: "Good night! It's all off!"

I suppose he meant the fight was all off. Assuredly the tuna was still on. Zee—zee—zee!

I bade him a mute and despondent farewell. But the line still held. It seemed to me that the thing which had to snap was in my head. I was nearly crazy. The making of angling history is sometimes painful. Zee—zee—zee! Slower and slower! Then, incredibly, when a couple of zees more would have pulled all the line out and broken it, the tuna stopped. The strain eased. He could not stand the pressure of water. He had started back. I wound and wound and wound that reel until I thought my arm would fall dead at my side. With a small reel it takes a great deal of winding to get in even a little line. This time it took perhaps half an hour to get all the line back. My tuna did not come readily all the time. He rested occasionally.

But I got him up, closer than ever before. He lazily rose to the surface about sixty feet or so from the boat. I heard him break water, but as the light was bad I could not see him. R. C. was on top of the deck. Captain Dan leaped up on the stern. They both saw the tuna. How strangely silent and tense they were! But I was too much exhausted and riveted to my post to have any thrills left. The tuna rolled around out there. He was a beaten fish. I realized it.

"Easy now," warned Captain Dan. "He's licked. Pull him along easy."

Then all of a sudden the reel stuck tight. The handle would not turn. The line would not run out. I could not tell Captain Dan. I was speechless. But he saw it. Quick as a flash he grasped a screw-driver and began to loosen the screws in the reel plate. How swiftly he worked! I heard him pant. My tuna was lolling around out there. Once I saw his saber-like tail and the size of it would have paralyzed me if I had not already been paralyzed.

Captain Dan got some of the screws loose. The spool grew less tight. One moment more and he would have the friction eased! But in that moment my tuna decided to loll and roll a little farther off, and he snapped the line. Five hours!

Some time afterward, when I was in condition to stand shocks, Captain Dan and R. C. both told me that they had seen the tuna, that he had been a beaten fish, and would have weighed at least a hundred and fifty pounds.

Tuna fishing has many poignant moments. Many as I have experienced, I never had but one as painful as this one I shall tell about, and how it was prolonged unenduringly.

It happened in late August. I had on board a guest, a publisher from New York, and I wanted him to hook a Marlin swordfish. R. C. was also with us, and last, though certainly not least, was my boy Romer, the irrepressible. Apparently the tuna season was ended. No boatman had seen tuna for days. We were convinced that the run of 1919 had passed into history. We steered off to the eastward toward San Diego and along the middle of the channel south, and finally turned west. We saw not a swordfish fin, nor a break on the surface. The sea was calm, dark blue, heaving and wonderful. The day was perfect. My friend grew tired of fishing and climbed up on deck to rest and invite his soul. There was just enough breeze blowing to ripple the water. I tired of fishing, also. R. C. was asleep. Romer was trying to fly a kite in the light wind. For a while I amused myself watching him. Then I watched the jellyfish. This season there had been a strange and remarkable run of jellyfish. The clear blue water seemed to magnify the rings and ropes and links and plaques of brilliant gelatinous matter. All of them had strings and spots of gold, of silver, of wondrous fire, in the center. The spots were the most exquisite violet, the intense color of a star seen through the telescope. The rolls clustered together, like coins, and in the center of each was the quivering electric

light. The sea was full of these floating jellyfish, from
tiny pieces to great coils twenty feet long. Seen deep
down they had a mysterious and weird appearance; seen
on the surface they were clear and transparent and beautiful. I had never seen anything like this before, nor had
Captain Dan in all his years at sea.

Once I happened to look up to the westward. Far
across the heaving blue on the horizon line I saw a white
spout of water. I peered more keenly. Another white
spout! Then another! I climbed up and stood on the
gunwale. I wanted to be sure before I woke anybody.
Plainly I saw more white spouts. Tuna! The sight
thrilled me through. Then farther to the westward, over
toward Clemente Island, I saw a white wall of water,
the greatest line of tuna I had ever seen.

Then I hailed Captain Dan. He took one look and
yelled: "There's a million of 'em! Wind in. We'll put
up the kite. An' we've got to hurry!" He slowed down
the boat and then got out the kite. It did not fly readily,
so he had to speed up the boat. I wound in my bait and
took off my leader. Romer immediately became interested in the approaching tuna. They looked to be at
least two miles distant, and the white wall had spread
across the channel, and many white splashes showed
closer to us. Suddenly I saw tuna dark and sharp in the
air against the blue horizon.

"Dan, look! By George! I believe that school is feeding!" I exclaimed.

"Feedin'? I should say so! They're drivin' the flyin'
fish offshore. You're goin' to see a sight pretty quick!"

Assuredly I warmed to the occasion. R. C. climbed up
on top and lifted the youngster after him. Captain Dan
needed me to help him with kite and bait, so I could not
look ahead. He let the kite up about three hundred
yards, broke the kite line, and gave it to me to hold.

[7]

Then he put a fresh flying fish upon my leader. This took time. It is a complicated job, this baiting a hook for tuna. When he had done this he tied my fishing line to the leader. Then, taking the kite line, he tied that at the juncture of my leader and fishing line. That done, he threw the bait overboard and told me to let out line. I let go of the reel and my line paid out. The kite soared, and lifted on my bait so that it skipped along the surface. I let out about a hundred yards. The kite swung my bait around at right angles with the boat, and when I jerked my rod a little, the bait would leap exactly like a live flying fish. We were now ready for the tuna, and I turned my head rather breathlessly.

R. C. and Romer were yelling. My friend was also exclaiming. They had reason to be delighted. Never had my eyes been greeted and gladdened by such a sight. Ahead of the boat, only a few hundred yards distant, the air was full of flying fish. High, low, everywhere, they were in wild flight. Behind them, for a mile across the channel, came the bursting white wall of water, and all over the ocean between us and this wall there were white boils and splashes, and hundreds of giant tuna in the air. Much as I had seen of tuna, I had never beheld this sight, surely the most wonderful to encounter on the ocean. Captain Dan had seen it but once, and not so great as this. I could hear the tumbling roar of water. I could hear the smashes and cracks where the huge fish curled on the surface, breaking water as they struck their quarry. Huge blue and green and silver flashes gleamed out of the wall of water. They were coming fast. Already the flying fish were around us, over us. They made a soft rustle in the air. We had to dodge them, but some hit the boat. They presented the most wonderful spectacle of frantic and terrified life, unable to escape the monsters of the deep. I had to feel pity for them. Their flight,

[8]

usually so regular and beautiful, so sailing and soaring, was now broken and wild. It seemed they did not dare alight. But of course they had to, for a flying fish cannot really fly. He leaps out and spreads his gauze-like fins and sails. When his momentum is lost he drops down with the long lower lobe of his tail in the water, and by a violent wiggling of his body he gets impetus for another flight.

Then the voracious school of tuna appeared to surround us. They closed all but one quarter of the circle, and that was to the east. They had no fear of the boat. The roar of the water was so loud that it sounded like the rapids of a river. The quick sharp cracks on the surface were like reports. A tuna rushes his prey, curls as he strikes, and literally smashes the water white. His speed, his power, his savage spirit, are indescribable. I saw dozens in the air at once, some small, mostly large, and now and then a huge one over two hundred pounds.

I forgot I was fishing. I did not think of the probability that in a moment I might have a tremendous strike. I was all eyes. But as I could not see all, I tried to see a little clearly. It was like trying to watch too many rings in the circus.

I saw a giant tuna swimming on his side, right under a flying fish that was in the air. I saw the great black staring hungry eye of the tuna as he shot past the boat. He made a bulge on the water, and by that bulge I followed him as he kept even with the poor flying fish until it fell. Then—smash! The water went furiously white in a ten-foot circle. I saw another tuna knock a flying fish high up into the air. I could see that the flying fish was crippled. And the tuna, so violent was his energy, went up and up fully fifteen feet, quivering and beautiful, an immense fish all blue and silver. The flying fish fell back before the tuna, and when the tuna fell back he made a lightning swift lunge at his luckless quarry. Again I saw a tuna not twenty feet astern of our boat come out in a long low leap, cutting the water till it hissed, and he took a flying fish in the air.

"Look out!" boomed Captain Dan. "There's one after your bait! Jump it! . . . Wow! No, he missed. . . . Look out, now—that tuna will go over two hundred!"

My wonderful spectacle had become alarmingly specific. The largest tuna I had seen was lunging at my bait. In my excitement I jerked it away from him. But it is impossible to jerk a bait altogether away from these swift monsters. He lunged again. I saw his back, dark blue and thick, his wide tail, so instinct with power. He made a splash as big as the stern of our boat. I jerked my bait. It shot right out of the jaws of this tuna. Then he went into the air as though from a catapult. The anger, the hunger, the beauty, the wild nature and terrible life expressed by that long round glistening fish simply made me gasp breathlessly. When my bait alighted he was there. He got it. And so tremendous was the strike that he broke the line.

"Wind in! Hurry! They're all around us," yelled Dan.

In less than a minute we had another bait overboard. The turmoil around us was now at its height. Fearfully I watched my bait as the kite dragged it across the foamy water. I had reason to gaze fearfully. That bait did not get forty feet away before a small tuna, verily the smallest in that vast school, hit it on the leap, hooked himself, and went down. My reel whizzed. The kite began to lower. Then the kite line broke and the kite soared up with a buoyant leap and sailed away.

The prolonged poignant moment was upon me. I was hooked to a small tuna, but he was large enough to hold me powerless for a while. And I had to sit there and hold the bobbing rod while that vast school of magnificent fish swiftly worked away from me. How swiftly I could see! The white wall and white patches and splashes on the water, the dark darting gleam of tuna, the cloud of flying fish in the air like a swarm of frightened bees, rapidly passed on to the south, and long before I had subdued the unappreciated fish on my line they were out of sight beyond the blue horizon.

II

GIANT NOVA SCOTIA TUNA

IT seemed a far cry from Avalon, California, to Liverpool, Nova Scotia. And at the beginning of the best
swordfish time on the Pacific, to leave for the doubtful pursuit of giant tuna off the Atlantic coast was something extremely hard to do. Had I not made plans a
year ahead, I probably would have taken the easy course
of postponement.

We were to find that the physical effort alone was
enough to daunt most anglers. The climate of Avalon
is the finest in the world. We had become used to cool
atmosphere with a tang of fog. The Pullman car was
a furnace; the Mojave Desert a glaring waste of hot rock
and sand; at Needles the mercury stood at 115 degrees.
Arizona gave us a most welcome respite and we reveled
in the green uplands of cedar and sage, the panorama of
clouds and dropping veils of rain, and rainbows curved
over the purple horizons. Kansas was dust and heat;
Chicago humid and muggy, and an infernal place of
noise and fury and gasoline; and not until we left Boston

to cross the Bay of Fundy did we get any rest and comfort.

An angler should not mind the discomforts of travel, weather, and crowds, but while these things are omnipresent, he has to think pretty hard of clear swift shady streams and limpid lakes and the cool heaving sea in order to convince himself that he is a rational being.

My plans of several years' development and a year of fixed purpose made it impossible to give up this Nova Scotia trip or regard it in any way except with thrilling zest.

Captain Laurie Mitchell of Liverpool, Nova Scotia, had inspired me to this undertaking. He had fought between fifty and sixty of these giant tuna, and had succeeded in catching one, the largest on record, seven hundred and ten pounds. This fish dragged him nine miles out to sea, and halfway back. It measured ten and one-half feet and was as large round as a barrel. J. K. L. Ross, another Canadian angler, who lives at St. Ann's Bay, has caught several of these great mackerel, all from four to six hundred pounds in weight. He, too, has lost at least seventy-five. Two others of these fish have been caught by an English angler, Mitchell Henry; and these few comprise the total that have ever been landed.

The game was a new one, with no very satisfactory method of pursuing it yet devised. Its possibilities seemed most remarkable. Its difficulties appeared almost as unsurmountable as broadbill swordfishing, though a great difference existed between these two strenuous types of angling.

I determined to go as fully equipped as was possible, and to try out the Nova Scotia method of fishing from a skiff, and also what I called a mixture of Florida and California methods.

[13]

Captain Mitchell had constructed for me two light skiffs, one eighteen and the other twenty feet in length, two-oared, sharp fore and aft, and round as a spoon on the bottom. My Florida boatman, Robert King, had a launch built for me in Fort Myers, following the model used by the skillful Florida mullet-fishermen. It was twenty-five feet long, seven and one-half beam, light and strong, and was equipped with two engines, two propellers and two rudders. It was guaranteed to make eighteen miles an hour, and turn round in its own length, at full speed. I had this launch shipped to Liverpool, with the special Catalina revolving chairs furnished with rod-sockets. One of each of these was to be installed in the launch and the two skiffs. Then I brought the tackles I had especially made for taking these great fish.

I was certain that these Coxe reels, Murphy hickory rods, and Ashaway linen lines were the very finest and most enduring which could possibly be built. This question of tackle is a most important one, and must of necessity come up often. Many bitter controversies have been waged by fishermen over the respective merits of light and heavy tackle. My contention has always been that the fair and sportsmanlike method is to use tackle strong enough to subdue the fish, and not to break off a number of hooked fish in endeavor to catch one on a lighter tackle. All hooked fish that break away become prey for sharks, or they die. The slogan of many anglers, "Lighter tackle, fewer fish!" is very impressive and fine-spirited to the inexperienced angler. But in this case the truth is this: "Fewer fish brought in to the dock, but many more dead in the sea!"

I was not yet in any position to write authoritatively about tackle and fishing for these enormous tuna, so many of which have been broken off. If hundreds of them have broken tackle and only about ten been caught, the per cent of loss runs very high. My swordfish tackle should be strong enough, provided the boat can be maneuvered very skillfully. But in any case, if this king of the mackerel family cannot be fairly beaten with the tactics I shall employ (and that means without breaking off many) I shall be inclined to give it up as a bad job. Sea fish no doubt grow too large to be whipped on any rod and reel. If the water is not shallow along this coast, so that it is impossible for tuna to sound, fishing for them with rod and reel would be ridiculous and cruel. It may be that anyway. But I have great hopes of finding it possible to consider this large tuna fishing in a class with broadbill swordfishing. No higher place could be given it.

At Yarmouth we encountered heavy fog, and to me it was like meeting an old friend from across the continent. Long before we ran into this lowering silver bank of fog I could smell it. Probably all fogs are alike. Surely they are all cool, wet, silent, strange, mysterious; and they hide everything from the sight of man. It is a fear-inspiring sensation to go driving over the sea through a dense fog. The foghorns, the whistles, the bell buoys all have a thrilling, menacing sound.

Here we disembarked and took a train, without being able to see what the port looked like. Some ten miles on we ran out of the fog into bright sunshine, and I found the Province of Nova Scotia to be truly of the northland, green and verdant and wild, dotted with lakes and areas of huge gray rocks, and low black ranges covered with spruce, and rivers of dark clear water.

As we progressed these characteristics enhanced. What welcome relief to eyes seared by sight of barren desert and hot cities! The long grass, the wild flowers, the dense thickets of spruce, the endless miles of green were a soothing balm.

Liverpool proved to be six hours' journey from Yarmouth, and turned out to be the very prettiest little town I ever visited. The houses were quaint and of an architecture unfamiliar to me, very inviting to further attention. Everywhere were huge trees, maples, ash, locusts, and they graced ample yards of luxuriant green. A beautiful river ran through the town, and picturesque fishing smacks lined its shores.

We were met by Captain Mitchell, and also my two boatmen, who had come on in advance. My party included my brother R. C. and my boy Romer and an Arizonian named Jess Smith. Out of these three I hoped to have a good deal of fun, besides the considerable help they could give.

We spent that afternoon unpacking our innumerable bags and grips and in trying out the Florida launch on the river. Bob King and Sid Boerstler, my boatmen, found out a good deal that did not suit them; and as often before, their incomparable value to me manifested itself. Sid held a high diploma for engineering ability, and Bob naturally and by long experience was an adept with tools, mechanics, and everything pertaining to boats. He had spent all his life fishing, living by the rivers and bays of Florida. He had a genius for catching fish. He made an art of it. They changed everything in that little launch. Nothing suited them. My boy Romer, who has begun to show marked interest in the mechanics of automobiles, hydroplanes, boats, and all manner of apparatus, had a very great deal to say about what should and should not be done, much to Bob's amusement. He said: "Romer, the trouble is this boat is all right, only it's wrong." To me Bob said: "That boy's smarter than an Everglade Indian."

[16]

Later that day we gave the launch a final try-out. I could not have hoped for more. It was fast, easy, comfortable, and could turn quicker than any boat I had ever been in. The self-starters worked admirably. It took about one second to get into motion. In fact, it started so abruptly that it threw me into a corner of the cockpit, and Jess nearly went overboard.

"Hey, cowboy," yelled Sid, testily, "trim the boat! This ain't a bronc!"

"Wal," drawled Bob, "she only makes aboot fifteen miles. She rides too high. The engines should have been forward. But I reckon we can chase these big tuna to a funeral."

Sid was even more pessimistic, mostly relating to the engines. He confounded me in technical complaint about gaskets, controls, levers, spark-plugs, and what not. Then at the conclusion of this tirade he added: "But she's pretty good. I'll soon have her so she'll ball the jack out of here like a scooter duck."

It is interesting to state, in passing, that Bob and Sid had a remarkable flow of language, highly edifying to me and a source of infinite amusement, but unfortunately most of it unprintable.

That evening we went down to the dock to see the native fishermen come in and unload their catch for the market. Docks are always fascinating places for me. This one appeared especially so. The brown river ran between green banks, with farms and cottages on the west side, and low rising piny hills beyond. On the town side a line of old weather-beaten storehouses stood back from the plank dock. You did not need to be told that Liverpool was a fisherman's town and very old. The scent of fish, too, was old, almost overpoweringly so. Two small schooners were tied up to the dock, the *Ena C.* and the *Una W.* What beautiful names are given to

Englishwomen and flowers and boats! One of these small ships, a two-master, had a crew of six, sturdy brown seamen, clad in rubber overalls. They had been out three days and had a catch of 16,000 pounds, codfish, halibut, and two swordfish. I surely had a thrill at sight of the broadbills. These were small fish compared with most I had seen during June and July on the Pacific. The codfish averaged twenty to thirty pounds. They had a number of halibut, several over two hundred pounds.

This schooner, with its weather-and-service-worn appearance, its coils of heavy hand-line, its skiffs dovetailed into one another, its rope and barrels and paraphernalia scattered about on the deck, and the deep hold from which the fishermen were pitchforking cod out on the dock, and the rude pulpit built out over the bowsprit, from which swordfish were ironed—all these held great interest and curiosity for me, filling me with wonder about the exploits of these brave simple men who lived by the sea, and emphasizing again the noble and elemental nature of this ancient calling.

We inquired to find out if any tuna had been seen lately. Several weeks ago, they told us, tuna had been plentiful in the bays and inlets. They had come with the first run of herring. But none had been seen lately. The first run of herring was earlier than usual. A big season was expected. Sometime round the middle of August the great mass of herring would arrive. These were the species that spawned along this shallow Nova Scotia shore. They were larger than the present fish. The schools of tuna followed them. We were a little early.

We engaged two natives to accompany us—Pence to run the large launch, and Joe to make himself generally useful. Both men knew the coast and all the fishermen.

Nova Scotia Herring Fishermen Marketing Day's Catch

PLATE V

Haddock (Finnan Haddie) Drying on the Racks

PLATE VI

Next morning we were up before five, and on the water in half an hour. When we turned the corner of high land, where the quaint white lighthouse stood, and I saw down the widening bay, I was charmed. The shore lines were rugged clean boulders that merged into the dark spruce forest. As we glided down the bay I saw green and black hills rising to a considerable height, and here and there white or gray cottages shone in the sunlight. Toward the mouth of the bay we entered the zone of the nets. They were stretched all along the shore, and the bobbing floats could be seen everywhere, from a quarter to a half mile out. We discovered several traps, which were likewise nets, but operated differently from the gill-nets. These had circles and lines of corks on the surface, marking the trap, and long wings leading off to each side. Captain Mitchell explained that the fishermen had just begun to put in their traps, and that around these the tuna would come and stay, and that was where there was the best chance of hooking one.

We ran up to one boat, to which two fishermen were hauling their gill-net. I saw herring shining in the water and being picked out of the net by the fishermen. We bought a bushel of them for chum and bait. This variety of herring was a beautiful little fish, nearly a foot long, shaped somewhat like a trout, only with smaller head, and colored brilliantly, dark green on the back, silver underneath, with sides that glowed opalescent. We proceeded along these nets, to a point opposite Western Head, a bold cape jutting out, and asked all the fishermen if they had discovered any tuna. But no one had seen any for over a week.

Then we ran outside the bay, round a picturesque lighthouse, into the ocean. I was amazed at the smooth, calm sea. R. C. and I could not believe our eyes. Was this the Atlantic? The gray old stormy sea we had

fought so long! Captain Mitchell assured us that it was
and that we would see many such fine days in this lati-
tude. There was no swell. The water scarcely moved.
The coast line appeared to be wonderfully indented by
bays and coves and inlets, and marked by beautiful
islands, dark with spruce, and bold headlands, rugged
and gray. Low clouds of fog shone white in the sun.
We ran through some of them, and between islands, and
along the shore for fifteen miles to a place called Cherry
Hill. Off this point Captain Mitchell had won his
memorable fight with his 710-pound tuna. We met and
talked with several net fishermen, none of whom had seen
any fish that day. So we ran out a few miles, and then
circled back toward Western Head. We sighted some
schools of pollack feeding on the surface, but no other
kind of fish. The sea remained tranquil all day, and
when we entered the bay again, late in the afternoon,
there was only a gentle ripple on the water. Then we
ran in, and so ended our first day, August 1st.

That night we heard of tuna having been seen ten
miles west, at Port Mouton, and decided to go there next
day. We made the same early start. The day equaled
the one before, and the shore line proved remarkably
beautiful. High wooded hills, green slopes, gray rough
banks, rose above the sea. We wound, at length, in between gemlike islands, where the channels were calm
and clear, and the round bays like glass, and the sandy
beaches burned white in the sunlight. Port Mouton was
a little fishing village with gray weather-worn houses
facing the sea. We landed at a dock where fishermen
were unloading tons of herring. Many of these were
being salted in barrels for lobster bait. It was a crude,
primitive place, singularly attractive with the weather-
beaten huts, boats, docks, its bronzed fishermen, its air
of quaint self-sufficiency. We were told that tuna had

been seen two days before off the island and eastward from the nets. There was a wreck that marked the locality. The leader of this fisherman squad talked interestingly:

"Our methods are crude," he said. "We have no money to buy proper equipment. We could do ten times as much. Herring fishing is but in its infancy. The supply is enormous and inexhaustible. The sea is a gold mine."

I agreed with him about the sea being a treasure house, but I could not believe the supply of herring inexhaustible. I had seen the bluefish, the menhaden, the mackerel, the white sea bass and albacore, all grow scarce where once they had been abundant. Herring, however, may be different. I heard of schools twenty miles in extent. In fact, I received an impression of the marvelous fecundity and vitality of this species. The whole south shore of Nova Scotia lived by the herring.

These fishermen called the tuna by the name of albacore. That was a surprise to me, for they certainly are not albacore. Horse-mackerel and tunny are two other names, characteristic of the Jersey shore and of the Mediterranean.

We found the place to which we had been directed, off a wild and lonely shore, where the ocean boomed and a great iron steamer, broken in the middle, gave grim evidence of the power of the sea in storm. The current was swift here. We anchored, and tried chumming for a few hours. But we raised no tuna. The wind came up strong and on the run back we sent the spray flying. The air grew chill. When the sun went under clouds I felt quite cold, despite my warm woolen clothes; and I was glad to get back.

Next day was Sunday. The Nova Scotians keep the Sabbath. They do not fish on the seventh day of the week. I am afraid they made me feel ashamed of my own lack of reverence. More and more we Americans drift away from the Church and its influence. Perhaps that is another reason for our lawlessness, our waning home life, our vanishing America. I should never forget that some of Christ's disciples were fishermen, and since then all fisher folk have been noted for their simplicity and faith. Liverpool was to awaken in me something long buried under the pagan self-absorption of life in the United States. When I was a boy I had to go to Sunday school and to church. It made me unhappy. I never could listen to the preacher. I dreamed, mostly of fields, hills and streams, of adventures that have since come true. As I grew older, and learned the joys of angling, I used to run away on Sunday afternoons. Many a time have I come home late, wet and weary after a thrilling time along river or stream, to meet with severe punishment from my outraged father. But it never cured me. I always went fishing on Sunday. It seemed the luckiest day. I do not consider it wrong. But I shall respect the custom of the Nova Scotians and stay quietly in the hotel on that day. Full well I know there will come a Sunday when the tuna will run into the bay and smash the water white.

Monday was cool and rather dark, with a southwest wind that made me favor the protected places in the sun. We anchored off Western Head, chummed and fished awhile, then ran out to sea several miles to try for halibut. About noon we returned and anchored in the bay opposite one of the traps, and tried again. The water grew rough and the wind cold.

Upon our return, rather late, we found most thrilling news awaiting us. All the herring fishermen are eager to help us find tuna and report every evening. One of them had three tuna under his boat all the time he was hauling his net. Two of the fish were very large. A *small* one usually runs about five hundred pounds. These tuna rushed for every herring that slipped away from the net.

Another fisherman found a hole in his trap, assuredly made by a big tuna. Then late this evening a third man reported seeing a large school of tuna near Coffin Island. All this is thrilling and exciting news. The presence of these great fish near at hand is something momentous. I have no idea how sight of one is going to make me feel. But it will be a tremendous experience. And to hook one—what will that be?

The weather is threatening to-night, cold, windy, dark, and the air seems storm-laden.

During the night I was awakened by the patter of rain on the roof. What a welcome sound to a traveler from California! The wind wrestled in the trees, moaned and soughed. I lay awake for a long while. Morning disclosed gray skies and copious showers. We had to forego our fishing. And we talked fish, tackle, past performances, especially those that concerned the tuna angling on the Nova Scotia coast.

Captain Mitchell had a hurry call on the telephone from Homans, a fisherman of Port Mouton. Homans sent information that tuna were thick in Jordon Bay, near Lockeport, some thirty miles from Liverpool. This was most alluring news. We decided to leave at once, sending the boats with the boatmen, and the rest of us traveling by auto. Meanwhile the skies cleared and the sun came out bright and warm. The ride down through the forest was both beautiful and hideous; it depended on where fire had been. Sable River attracted my fisherman's eye. It was a rock-lined, hemlock-shaded stream of clear dark water, almost black. The driver said it contained fine trout.

As we neared Lockeport I caught glimpses of the ocean, and a blanket of white fog far out, drifting toward shore. That worried me. I was afraid the boats would have to put in.

The fishing settlement, a small town, was located on an island to which we crossed over a bridge, and it was surrounded by islands, little and big, and a ragged stretch of mainland, where the breakers crawled foaming up the rocks. I heard the melancholy wash of the surf, and presently espied a beautiful curved beach of sand, very broad and smooth, upon which little lines of shallow breakers rolled.

We found comfortable quarters, and at once set out to learn something about the tuna. We were overjoyed to find out that Jordon Bay was full of tuna. Many had gotten into the nets and a few had been harpooned. There was no market for them here. Our design to catch tuna on rod and reel excited no little interest.

After supper we went out to be surprised and dismayed to find the fog had drifted in. It was not heavy, but it obscured the sea and islands, and gradually the houses at a distance. I was discouraged. What was worse, we received a telephone message from Port Mouton informing us that our boats had to put in there on account of the fog.

Just before dark young Romer disappeared. We looked everywhere for him, and at last Jess found him way out on one of the fish docks, all by himself. Jess said: "By golly! it was so foggy I couldn't see very far. Nearly fell off the dock. I yelled and he answered. Then I found him fishing. He had caught fifty-seven pollack, several as long as his arm, and he was shore excited. He was throwing them back. He made me stay long enough to catch one myself. I reckon Romer is a chip off the old block."

That sort of pleased me. Romer had been rather trying with his incessant energy and mischievousness. The fish dock had to be approached by narrow alleys, running round behind fish houses and big gloomy buildings. It was a lonesome and a weird place, shrouded as it was in thin fog. I would not have cared to spend any time there. I certainly marked this incident down to the lad's credit.

Before going to bed I walked out upon the porch. The little fishing hamlet was wrapped in silence and gray obscurity. No lights showed. A few dim shapes of houses loomed darkly. Somehow it was oppressive. To think these people lived here, half the time unable to see across the road!

Morning brought no change. A heavy fog mantled the port. There was no help for it. My impatience and eagerness must be endured. About eight-thirty the fog lightened somewhat and a pale sun, just visible, shone through. I went down to the dock.

It was a bustling place. The herring boats were coming in from the nets to unload the morning's catch. Some boats were half full of the beautiful silver-green and pink fish; others had not so many, and some only a few bushels. These boats and the fishermen who manned them certainly showed the labor and travail of their calling. Yet how picturesque they seemed! The men were hardy, rough, genial, clad in rubber, covered with fish scales, and redolent of the sea. The wharf where they discharged their cargo was a busy scene, just as hard and crude as their boats. I was tremendously interested to see what became of the herring. Since the magnificent tuna fish followed the herring, lived off them, the same as the fishermen, I wanted to know all that was possible about them.

Information obtained from H. R. L. Bill, owner of the fish market, Lockeport, Nova Scotia:

Kippered herring are shipped mostly to upper Canada and Vancouver—season starts in September.

New York handles a lot of Scotch cured herring with the heads on—cheap way of preparing. They are stripped, only insides removed, not split, and salted—60 pounds of salt to the barrel. Also called Matjes herring—much used by Jews in New York.

Kippered herring are pickled for one hour—smoked one night— only 24 hours old when smoked. 9x18 ft. smoke house—six fires of hard wood and sawdust—smoked one night on racks in the ceiling.

Split herring—Fat herring are best in July—cured 10 days, packed filled with salt.

No. 1 herring are eleven inches and up.

July and August are the hot months in the United States and when there is most fog. Fog caused by the warm waters of the Gulf Stream coming into the cold water of the Atlantic.

About one hundred small motor boats have lain about the wharf at Lockeport, laden with cod, at one time. Usually eighteen vessels a day in winter—able to fish only about one day a week in winter.

Lockeport, Nova Scotia. Information from H. R. L. Bill on fish and fishing:

Most winter fish are shipped fresh—what they can't ship are made into fillets—also the small "scrod"—all kinds of small fish are made into fillets and salted down.

The "pine-tree cod" are caught in the fall on the shoals. They have a design on their sides that looks like a pine tree.

Fish caught on kelp bottom are red cod and other fish caught in shoal water are yellow.

One day 15,000 pounds of halibut were boxed on Mr. Bill's wharf in one morning.

The town of Lockeport handles 5,000,000 pounds of cured fish in one season.

It takes 360 pounds of fresh fish to make one cantle (112 lbs.).

Sixty pounds of smoked finnan haddie are obtained from one hundred pounds of fresh haddock.

Thirty-five pounds of fillets from one hundred pounds of fresh fish.

Two boxes of dried herring (40 fish each) from one bushel.

One barrel of split herring from four and one-half bushels.

They use ocean salt—Mediterranean. The best is from Trapenay (an island off the coast of Italy).

Bill's firm uses 10,000 bushels of salt. West Indian salt also used—from Turk's Island. Trapenay salt contains no lime, but West Indian salt does. Therefore the former is best for fish.

I met some of these fishermen, all of whom were eager to give me information or help me to succeed. Most of them were doubtful. All were sure I would hook many tuna. But to land one on a rod was improbable. They told me about ironing (harpooning) these monsters and fighting them on a rope. Their boats would be towed for miles, at first very swiftly. One fellow lost five tuna in succession the same morning. Another had a tuna that broke through all the nets in the bay and finally got loose.

"The albacore are there," said another. "I saw some and heard a lot of them this morning. Splashing round the nets. It was too foggy to see clearly."

I talked with the native fisherman who was Whitney's guide when he fought a large tuna. It whipped him and also his comrade. They chased it around until it lodged on a rock, and finally the boatman harpooned it.

At four o'clock Captain Mitchell and my boatmen arrived to report a most difficult trip from Port Mouton. They had to follow the buoys, and finding each one in the dense fog was no easy matter. We planned to go to Jordon Bay to-morrow, in any event.

To-night, about six, the fog settled down so thick it could be cut. It was heavy, wet, and most depressing to a Californian. I could not accustom myself to the gloom, the spectral shapes, the silence, the dampness, the inscrutable mystery. I love the fog in California, but this Nova

Scotia brand is another matter. I can hear the drip, drip, drip of heavy drops on the porch outside, the low sad wash of the surf, and the moan of a distant fog whistle. Yet somehow all this is thrilling. Contrasts are helpful. I cannot understand how people could choose to live in a country where fog predominated over sunshine, but it serves to make me appreciate my own country vastly more.

Next morning Lockeport was so thickly muffled that you could not distinguish one house from another. Hours we wandered round, waiting. It was most trying. Never before had I known what it meant to be fog-bound. About ten o'clock it lifted enough for us to see the wharves, the boats, and some of the capes, all dim and weird. We decided to run to East Jordon Bay, some eight miles round the headlands. This was a dangerous passage even in fair weather, for anyone who did not know the coast. Some of the fishermen disclaimed any wish to pilot us. Finally one of the dealers let us have his skipper, a man who had navigated this coast for twenty years. With him we set out. In ten minutes we lost sight of the town and could see only a few rods all around us. Sid and Bob, with R. C., kept close behind in the launch. Sometimes we could not discern the rocky bluff. I could hear the wash of the sea when the land was invisible. Occasionally dim slopes loomed up ahead. I could see them grow out of the gray gloom. How indistinct and far away they seemed! But they were close. Rocks! Ugly, jagged rocks, they looked like sea demons rising out of the water to smash us. We managed to elude them. Beyond we encountered a heavy swell. Our boats rocked and tossed. Soon I could hear the mournful whistling-buoy. Bob called it, "Groaner," and indeed that was felicitous. Soon a dark wall loomed through the fog. It was the headland we had to pass.

The sea boomed against it. I could see the dim white breakers dash upon it, and climb. What a frightful place to pass! Suppose our engine went dead! We would have been lost. When we rounded that forbidding point, begirt with thundering surges, it was none too soon for me.

Inside the bay the water was calm and the fog thinner. Several times we saw land, and one of these points was Blue Island. It towered like a mountain. We traveled on for an hour or more, and finally reached a ruined lighthouse and a dilapidated breakwater. Through the fog I discerned the dim outline of a house, and boats, and net racks. This was East Jordon. We tied up to the dock.

A fisherman named Sears lived there. He and his men kept a weir, for the purpose of catching herring. He was a huge man and looked the lifetime he had spent there. He said the bay was full of albacore and that two had been caught in the weir the day before. He expected the weather to clear. Naturally we were cheered, and we waited another two hours until the fog lifted somewhat. A breeze sprang up, rippling the bay. Across from us rose a wooded ridge, wild and ragged, and behind us sloped a verdant farm, with a generous sprinkling of evergreens.

We ran out with the two boats to a point halfway between the shores, and anchored the big boat, to which we tied. Then we began to chum. The herring ground to bits made a slick in the water. It drifted away across the bay, toward the weir. The breeze strengthened until there was a noticeable ripple. I was watching a dark shadow on the water, wondering what it was, when R. C. and Bob yelled in unison: "Tuna! Tuna!"

I nearly fell off my seat. The dark shadow had been a school of fish. We all yelled at the sight of fins. Slim

dark sharp fins unmistakably those of tuna. The fish did
not show well nor long. After that we kept on chumming. Soon Bob sighted a second school coming down
the bay. It crossed the slick, to our great excitement.
But nothing happened. The slick did not hold them.
I was the lucky one to sight the third school of these huge
fish. Two more schools followed, and not one of them
paid any attention to our chum. Finally when we were
out of chum and had left only a few herring for bait, I
decided to troll before these tuna, after the manner in
which we feed a bait to a swordfish.

We had no difficulty getting in front of a school, although they swam swiftly. We ran beyond them and
stopped the engines of the launch. Bob began to throw
herring in front of the tuna. Suddenly the water roared.
It seemed a swirling hole sucked down a herring. Frantically I wound my bait to get it near. We all shouted.
But the tuna did not take another bait.

Then, after that school disappeared, we ran around
searching for another. It did not take long to find one.
We tried the same method, which this time did not work
so well. But a third school gave us a better chance, and
again we saw the huge swirl as one of the giant mackerel
took a bait. R. C. and Bob wished for a kite to fly, after
the Pacific method of getting a bait to tuna, but Sid and
I were at first rather doubtful about the possible success
of that.

At last we had to quit, owing to lack of bait. Moreover, the fog had begun to shut down. We ran back to
the breakwater and held a council of war. I had sent
for two cars to meet us at this point, and had intended to
return to Liverpool that night and have the boats follow
as soon as permitted by fog. But now I decided to send
R. C. and Jess and the boy back, and remain myself.

They left at four-thirty, with the understanding that

they were to return the next day with food supplies and some camping equipment. I walked up and down the long breakwater, hungry and tired. We had little to eat, and nothing that I wanted.

Between six and seven o'clock the fog lifted again, so that we could see objects low down. One of the native fishermen was out in a skiff to look into the weir. For the first time then I paid some attention to this contraption. When he rowed back and shouted, "Two albacore in the weir!" I was tremendously excited.

Sid and Bob rowed me out to the weir. It had a long wing reaching out from the bank two hundred yards or more. The construction was simple, consisting of thin saplings of spruce driven down into the mud. They were a foot apart, and at the low-tide level and also high-tide level were pieces nailed crosswise for strength. No wire or net of any kind! This long wing led out to a large heart-shaped corral open at the apex for about fifteen feet. Then from the other side of this corral extended a large wing, curved deeply back toward the straight line and working away from it. The corral was built after the same fashion, of saplings a foot apart. There was nothing else to stop the fish. Herring and mackerel could have swum through these fences as easily as through unobstructed water. But the strange fact was they did not. A school of herring would come down with the tide, strike the wing, and follow along it to enter the mouth of the heart-shaped corral. Then they would circle to the left. They would keep on circling and circling until the men came out with a net and surrounded them with it. I could scarcely believe fish were so stupid. As for tuna staying in that place—I scouted the idea.

We rowed round the inclosure of thin poles, very curious and skeptical. Suddenly Bob yelled: "Wow! Look at that boil!"

Then I saw an enormous swirl and an eddying of the water such as could only be made by the tail of a powerful fish. We stood up in the skiff, and clinging to the poles we peered through, as if we were watching for a tiger. Twice more the big swirl appeared.

"He's thar," vociferated Bob, "an' he's a humdinger. They'll ketch him easy. Funny about fish in a trap. They're all alike except mullet. You can't keep mullet millin' round."

It was an astounding thing for me to ascertain there was really a tuna inside that weir and he would not go out the way he came in. When we saw the fishermen rowing out in their big sharp-nosed yawls we went round the weir beyond the curved wing to meet them. Sears invited us to go inside to see the fun.

"There's not much money in it for us," he said, "but we got to keep the albacore out of the weir, else the herring won't come in. Sometimes we drive one out. We're going to kill these and ship them."

We remained just outside the mouth of the heart-shaped corral, while the fishermen fastened their net to the left side, and then began pulling the boat round by holding to the poles. They let the net out of the boat as they worked round. Big corks kept the top of the net afloat.

"Sometimes a smart albacore will hug the poles and we'll fail to get him in the net. Then we have to try over. We made six hauls the other night, before we got one."

When they had half circled the inclosure and had drawn the net away from the opening, we rowed inside. Presently they joined the ends of the net and hauled the purse strings. That closed the net at the bottom. The circle of corks was now perhaps fifty feet in diameter. Sears kept to the outside in his boat, while his three men fastened their boat to the weir and gradually drew in the net, narrowing the circle. Suddenly I saw a blue flash in the middle of the net circle. It was followed by a roar in the water and a tremendous white splash. We were fully fifty feet back, yet the splash reached us.

"Got a netful!" yelled Sears, above the sound of thumping water.

We rowed closer, and I stood up to see better and to take pictures. The inside of that net then became a threshing cauldron. I could make out huge fins and blue gleams and silver flashes. Presently by looking deep in the water I could see a tuna plunge against the net, then slide along. He gleamed like an enormous silver-green shield. The tuna had no room to get headway. It looked easy for them to leap out or slide over the net, but not one made the attempt. As the net was drawn closer and closer the mêlée increased, and for a few moments there was a tremendous splashing.

"They'll give up quick," said Sears. "Sometimes, though, we get hold of a fighter. Not long ago one sank our boat, tore through the net and got away."

I hoped these would all escape. It was an exciting and painful spectacle for me. Presently the fury of plunging eased and then I could see the huge fish piling over one another. Their round backs were like barrels. They lifted their great heads out and gaped with wide mouths. The action was really a gasp. Soon they were so constricted that they could only roll, and beat with mighty tails.

"Only four of them," said Sears. "I thought there were more. They'll give up soon now."

Indeed it seemed so, except in case of the largest. The folds of the net meshed them so they could hardly move. Then two of the fishermen stood up in the skiff. One was armed with a mattock having a spike fully a foot long.

The other had a huge mallet, almost too heavy to swing,
I thought. It sort of paralyzed me to see these two men
prepare for action. What Bob and Sid said was funny,
but would not do for publication. When one of the
huge tuna rolled his head out the man with the mattock
struck him, imbedding the iron several inches in his head.
Then the man with the mallet drove the iron mattock
clear to the end. It took five powerful strokes. Then
they served two more of the tuna in the same way. The
water turned red. This work seemed on the moment
a horrible butchery to me. It made me sick. Those
wonderful beautiful fish!

"Well, it's their country and their work," said Bob,
meditatively, as if trying to excuse it to himself. "They
have to keep this trap clear for the herring."

The fourth and largest tuna did not give up. Scarcely
had his three companions been dispatched when he began
to beat with his tail. Faster and faster! He carried net
and boats away with him. The roar of water was like
that from a huge propeller. He churned a space half as
large as the inside of the weir. The yells of the men and
their strenuous efforts to hold him proved the resistance
of that fish. But they drew the bag of the net closer
and closer until he was rolled up in it, and then hauling
him to the surface they mattocked and malleted him to
death.

Then the fishermen towed their catch ashore and tied
them in shallow water. The last act of the day was to
chop open their throats with an ax, so they would lose
all their blood.

"Wal, them albacore are stupid as pigs an' they shore
get treated like pigs," was Bob's last comment.

We rowed back to the boats. I did not eat any supper.
I walked the long breakwater from the lighthouse to the
shore. The fog shut down thick and wet. It seemed a

MARKET FISHERMEN CLEANING HERRING

PLATE VII

MARKET FISHERMEN NETTING TUNA

PLATE VIII

gloomy hard place, with none of the charm of the south. There were teeth in this northland country. At dark I crawled into one of the little bunks and went to sleep. Several times during the night I awoke, cold and wet. At intervals I heard the low strange moan of the whistling-buoy at the mouth of the bay six or eight miles out. It seemed to harmonize with the surroundings.

At dawn the fog was thicker than ever. We could not see fifty feet. Moreover, we heard the rumble of thunder. A storm was coming down on us. The thunder grew heavier, and at last lightning penetrated the thick mist. What a ghastly phenomenon—lightning-illuminated fog! Then it began to rain. It poured. And gradually the deluge beat down the fog, so that we could see the land with its dark fringe of spruce trees. It rained for three hours, then let up to some extent, so that we could get out and move round.

And presently we took the boats and made for the middle of the bay. The water was dead calm, except where ripples and wrinkles and waves showed the presence of tuna. All the bait we had been able to procure was a bushel of small herring, not very good for our needs. But we used them, anyway. We chummed, and I sat with a bait out. Then it began to rain, and it rained hard for two hours. All this while I sat there hoping for a strike. I got cold and wet, though I had on heavy woolen clothing and rubber coat. The fog drifted by to quell the rain; then the rain clouds got the upper hand of the fog. At last we used up our bait. We ran back to the breakwater, where I dried my clothes and shoes by the little stove in Captain Pence's boat. The rain pattered on the roof. At two o'clock it ceased and all around the fog curtain lifted. For the first time I saw down the bay to Blue Island and Gull Rock, and then on to West Headland. The scene was superb.

I had three hours to wait for the car that was to come for me. So quite naturally I decided to get some bait and fish some more. We took the launch and crossed the bay and ran down six or seven miles. We sighted some fish-net buoys, then some storehouses on the shore, and finally fishermen. Here we obtained a bushel of herring that had just been salted. With these we proceeded to where the schools of tuna had been sporting. Sure enough, they were still there.

We planned to work in front of a school and beyond it, then stop the engines. I was to throw my bait out, and the boys were to throw herring. The very first school of tuna presented favorably. I could see four or five fish, tails and dorsals out, but there were surely a dozen or more in this school. The leaders pushed waves a foot high ahead of them. They made identically the same waves as the Pacific tuna, only larger. What a thrill I had as they came on! I could hear the soft swish of the water.

When the leaders were perhaps fifty feet from the launch I pitched my bait fully halfway to them. Then Bob and Sid threw out herring. I saw a wide slow swirl, then a rising wave.

"He's got your bait!" yelled Bob.

Quick as a flash I leaped down to straddle my rod and grasped it. The line whizzed off the reel. I meant to let the fish take time with the bait. But he let go. Instantly I saw my mistake. Had the drag of the reel been set that tuna would have hooked himself!

"You should have soaked him," said Bob. "Say, but he was quick. I saw him take that bait. He'd have hooked himself. Some fish, I'll tell the world!"

My bait was the only herring taken by this school. Much excited and encouraged, we hunted for more tuna. We ran from one bunch to another, and sometimes consumed moments in heading the leaders, and we tried to work the same method that had earned my first strike from a Nova Scotia tuna. We had no more such luck. We counted four herring taken by tuna, but not one of these baits had my hook in it. At last we drove them all down for the time being, and once more the fog set in, lowering, drab, cold, dismal. I was in a glow of excitement and had forgotten mist, rain, everything but tuna. It was after four o'clock and the car was waiting for me. I left the boats there and started for Liverpool, with the intention of coming back next day. The farther I rode from East Jordon the clearer grew the weather, and at Liverpool the sun was shining and clouds were all golden. R. C. and Romer listened to my story with bated breath.

"We're going to catch one of those birds," avowed Romer.

I wondered, and felt a rush of thrilling hope, tinctured by doubt. When I remembered the majestic motion of that grand tuna, his swift yet ponderous action, the vast shining green-silver bulk of him, and the swirling waves he shoved ahead of him, I was only a humble and longing fisherman.

On Sunday afternoon we left Liverpool for East Jordon, and had a different and more entertaining ride through wide country, woods and moose meadows, and thick brush. We emerged from this at Jordon Falls. From that point to the lighthouse on the bay was only a short run.

The sun had shone all afternoon, up until now, and at four o'clock the fog began to roll in. Joe reported sighting numerous tuna around the weir on Saturday, but none on Sunday. After supper I walked along the lonely beach, and could not see far through the gloom. The shore was lined with huge gray boulders and fringed with stunted spruce trees. The time and place were not conducive to cheer.

R. C. and I made our beds in the launch, there being just room for one cot and a bed on the floor. We both slept well. At five o'clock all was mantled in thick gray fog. We could not see the lighthouse from the shore. We had breakfast, and then there seemed only waiting. But at seven-thirty I decided to go in the launch after herring. We towed the skiff, and crossed the bay in the fog. Finally we saw shore, and soon encountered several fishermen, from whom we bought a barrel of bait. One of them said there ought to be tuna at his nets, and I hired him to go with us. One of his companions went also, which made us eight in the launch. Too many! As we ran down the bay the fog began to whiten and thin. Soon we saw net-buoys, then Gull Rock, and at last Blue Island. The sun shone pale through the fog. I began to reproach myself for complaints that the fog would never lift.

We found the fisherman's nets full of herring, and Romer and Joe began to pick herring from the meshes. They were still alive, caught behind the gills. Presently another fisherman came along in his boat and told us he had just been feeding herring to a big albacore round his net. I hired him to take us over there and to stand by.

The distance was short. Soon we were tied to the net-buoy and chumming. I put a bait over, rather with a feeling that there was not much chance of a tuna coming along. But in less than five minutes I had a terrific strike, and I jerked with all my might, yelling: *"Strike! Strike!"*

Excitement reigned on that boat. The tuna lunged, dragging my tip into the water, and he ran off away from that net toward another. Sid had the engines going and we were after him with wonderful quickness. I could not believe that I was hooked to a tuna. My legs shook as they used to shake years ago when I had my first swordfish experiences. But gradually I recovered, and as we went after the fish, and I pumped and wound in line, there was hilarity added to the excitement on board. The tuna ran round a net-buoy and fouled the line. I loosened the drag, then while the boys frantically endeavored to free my line the tuna went off on his first terrific rush. He took two hundred yards off the reel. Suddenly I felt my line free of the buoy. Bob had cut the rope on the buoy. We were free, and away we sped after him! The fisherman followed in his launch.

There was sunshine around us, and the shore glimmered through fog. I fought this fish pretty hard while he was taking us up the bay. Sometimes he towed us. The little launch handled perfectly. We were a wildly excited crowd. I endeavored to calm myself and to face the fact that the tuna would probably get away.

Meanwhile the sun came out and we could see everywhere. It was beautiful alongshore. The fish had taken us four miles up the bay. In an hour he appeared to be slowing down and getting tired.

Then he made for shore. Ugly rocks stuck up all around us. The fisherman was of the opinion the tuna had gone in there to cut the line on the rocks. But I did not take this seriously.

R. C. stood up on the bow, and presently he yelled: "I see him! A whale! He'll go five hundred!"

This at once terrified and elated me. I worked as hard as I could. The tuna kept ahead of us, and he turned every way. The leader got tangled round his tail. At first we welcomed that, as we thought it would soon exhaust him. But it did not. He swam near the surface and kept among the rocks. Once Captain Mitchell said: "We'd better lead him out of here." But he would not lead, and we followed him round. When he swam quickly to one side, dragging the line under the boat, I jumped up, threw off my drag, and poked my rod down in the water clear to the reel. I had not yet realized the hazardous position into which the fish had dragged us. I was not worried. In fact I had begun to feel he was weakening and that I would get him.

It began to dawn upon me presently that there was something most unusual and sinister in the action of this fish, turning and wheeling for the rocks. I could not see those rocks deep under the surface, but I heard the boys yell: "Look out! Slack off! Rocks! Starboard!" and various other alarms. When, however, the fish ran straight for a black-nosed reef that was wreathed in foamy breakers, then I gave way to panic. We turned and tacked this way and that. Time after time the big mackerel ran under the boat, and I had to leap up, throw off my drag, and plunge the rod into the water. Seven times I did this successfully. But it was risky business. We followed him in and out, round the black rock, through channels, over shoals, and toward the beach. Then he swept out a couple of hundred yards. I began to breathe easier. But my relief was short-lived. Again he made for the rocks.

"Say, we're following him too much!" shouted R. C.

That warning fell upon deaf ears, for still I had no consistent fear he would cut off on the rocks. We got in a bad position, nearly sliding upon a flat rock we had not seen. The tuna went round it and we had to navigate between the rock and the breakers in order to free the line.

"Go to it!" I yelled, above the roar. "We can swim if we have to!"

Romer, whose face I happened to see, was white and rapt, perfectly wild with excitement and joy. He kept shouting advice to me. R. C. looked stern and grim as he stood up on the bow and waved Sid to steer to port or starboard. Once he called to me, "Good night!" and pointed to a green curling breaker with its white crest. How it boomed! Fifty feet in shore! With the tuna going strong! Still something happened to save us, and we ran round the bad rock away from the heave of the swell that raced toward the ledge. I had a few moments of comparative relaxation.

But when the stubborn tuna deliberately swerved back for the rocks I realized that he was not lunging for shoal water by accident. He had tried every means in deep water to dislodge the infernal thing that held him, and failing, he had headed for the rocks. How strange I had not believed this before! But it was hard to fight the fish and think deliberately at the same time. I had called these giant tuna stupid, an accusation made without careful consideration, and I was now compelled to retract it. At least this tuna was keen, cunning, resourceful, and probably unbeatable. It was instinct that guided him.

Suddenly he made a quick surge on the surface. I saw him—huge, blue-moving mass! It shook my heart, that sight. He swept round, and again the line went under the bow. I leaped up, and threw off my drag. Too quick! As I plunged my rod down into the water I saw some loops of slack line drift back toward the tip. I was frightened. I feared they would catch on the guides. They did catch. I felt a powerful pull—then the rod shot up. My line had caught on the tip and cut off on a guide!

Perhaps I had suffered more at the loss of a great fish —years ago. But not lately. I was stunned. Poor Romer looked sick. R. C. swore roundly and said we had bungled by letting the fish stay in the shallow water. For my part I did not see how we could have helped that.

[41]

Bob thought we might have dragged him, turned him. And so did Captain Mitchell. We saw him twice after he was free, a blur of blue, moving ponderously away. I felt weak and had a nausea.

"Two hours and ten minutes!" reckoned R. C. "And you had him coming! Rotten luck!"

"Well, it was my fault," I replied, finally. "There's nothing to do but swallow it—and try again."

We made our way back to the point between Gull Rock and Blue Island. It was clear and sunny now. What a magnificent view! I put R. C. on the rod to try his luck, and I rested and watched. I was wet with sweat and somewhat shaken by emotion. All the preparation and thought could not do less than have me roused to a high degree of feeling.

The sea was running high, with big swells and waves, yet it was not uncomfortable. Gull Rock, a bare gray steep rock, was chafed by contending tides. Blue Island was a long wild strip of timbered land, with a bluish color. Far beyond, the great white rollers dashed upon West Head, and across the bay on the other headland rose the white spire of a lighthouse. Fishermen were working at their nets. Up the bay the green and gray shores smiled under a belated sunshine, and the cottages of the fishermen stood out upon the hills.

"There's a tuna!" yelled R. C.

I came to with a jump, just in time to see a swirl in our slick. We waited with beating hearts. R. C. sat rigid, ready to strike back, should one of these giants take hold. But nothing happened.

We did not see any more tuna, and used up most of our herring. Then we ran up the bay to try again. We chummed another hour. R. C. sighted a tuna, Captain Mitchell another. They were isolated fish. Evidently no schools were running. So at five o'clock we came ashore.

After resting awhile and having supper I found I was pretty tired. My arms and wrists ached. My head ached, too. It appeared then that I had worked harder on this fish than I realized at the time. We talked over the whole event from all angles, and we certainly marked our mistakes. Mine seemed the most inexcusable. Yet how swiftly it had happened! And that was the first time such a thing had ever happened to me.

By way of a happy change we had the first clear late afternoon, with breeze in the west, and that in itself meant much to me.

Toward sundown I noticed signs of an unusually vivid promise of color in the west. And I wandered out to the end of the long breakwater and sat beneath the old deserted lighthouse. Sure enough, the sunset was beautiful, the first I had seen in Nova Scotia. The west appeared to be sheeted over with a belt of clouds and these all turned from rose to flaming red. It made a glorious blaze over water and land, until the whole world seemed on fire. The freshness and vividness of the color struck me singularly. It took some of the somberness and the cold hard gray quality out of this northland. I watched it until the shadows of dusk at last subdued the afterglow.

Next morning I was up at four-thirty. There were gray clouds in the east and patches of sky, colorless, like the hue of a moonstone, very soft and misty. The air was cool, sweet, damp, laden with mingled scent of sea and forest. How strange to have my view unobstructed by fog! Far down the bay I could see the points of the headlands, and two islands, one large and one small, that I at once recognized, though I had not seen them at this distance. We had breakfast at five o'clock.

When we came out again the east was a wonderful delicate gold, too exquisite to attempt to describe.

Soon we were off down the bay, the launch leading the way to pick up the native fisherman who had piloted us to his nets. The water was as level as a mirror and as reflective. The delicate gold suffused all the soft misty clouds, growing stronger as I watched, until at length the sun burst forth gloriously, a golden fire, bathing forest, bay, and meadow slopes in a wondrous luster. Fire at sunset and gold at sunrise! After all the gloomy foggy weather I had been rewarded. It gave me such a different feeling toward this rugged land of seashore and rock-ridged forest.

In less than half an hour we had reached the first of the nets, and soon after that arrived at a point between Gull Rock and Blue Island where the morning before I had hooked my first tuna. How different a scene now! Gentle heaving sea, sparkle of water, bobbing boats of fishermen lifting their nets, the tang of salt, fresh from the vast open space beyond, the clear outline of Gull Rock, a desolate, forbidding gray stone, the swelling rise of Blue Island, green and dark, and bathed in sunrise gold, and then out over the promontories a low belt of land fog—these met my roving glances and gave me the delight that makes so much of the worthiness of fishing and the good fortune which befalls the early angler.

We procured a basketful of herring from the fisherman who had accompanied us down the bay. Then we ran on to the next fisherman, who had seen one tuna about his net, but not for some time. Nevertheless we tied on to his buoy and began to grind chum and throw out herring. I put a bait over and waited with my heart in my throat. One tuna strike had prepared me for a second.

"Look down there!" exclaimed Captain Mitchell.

"By Jove! that fisherman is punching at a tuna near his boat."

It did seem so. I saw the man strike with an oar, saw the splash, and then when he poised, as if waiting for another chance to hit something, I yelled out:

"Let's get there pronto."

And in less time, almost, than it takes to tell it we were on our way. Captain Pence, however, with R. C. and Romer on board the large boat, did not follow at once.

We ran straight down on the fisherman we had watched and hauled in close.

I made eager query: "Didn't we see you hit at a fish?"

"Yes. There are two albacore round; one of them's a big one. He was stealing herring almost out of my hands."

We explained our intentions and asked if we could tie to his buoy. He nodded, and grinned when he said he hoped we would hook on to the big one.

No doubt of our excitement! The certainty of a strike made it impossible to be calm. In less than two minutes I was holding tenaciously to my rod and watching the shiny slick float down along the net.

"Bad place to hook one, if he runs up the bay," warned Captain Mitchell, pointing to the net-buoys. Indeed the lane between them was tortuous and narrow. My feeling was one of dismay at that prospect; my hope was that if I hooked one he would run out to sea.

"*Oh-h!*" yelled Sid, hoarsely, in most intense excitement. At the same instant I heard a tremendous splash. Wheeling, I saw white and green water settling down near the net, not fifty yards from us.

"That was a tuna!" exclaimed Captain Mitchell. "Did you hear the smash? He was after a herring."

Sid jabbered like a wild man, until finally I made

something of his speech: ". . . big blue tuna! He had a back like a horse! He came half out!"

Bob's eyes flashed like keen blue fire. "I saw him. Some he-scoundrel, that fish!"

"You'll get a strike in no time," added Captain Mitchell. "If only he doesn't run up the bay!"

My state was one of supreme rapture, dread, and doubt combined. I really was not a rational being. There I sat, left hand holding about four feet of loose line off my reel, my right clutching the rod, my eyes everywhere. I saw the net, the slick, the drifting particles of chum Bob was grinding, the shiny floating herring Captain Mitchell threw in, the bright green water, the buoys and boats and fishermen. R. C. and Romer sat perched upon the deck of their boat, perhaps a quarter of a mile distant. Romer was watching us through glasses. How long would I have to wait? Five minutes seemed an age.

Suddenly the loose line whipped out of my hand and ran through the guides on the rod.

"There!" I whispered, hoarsely.

My line swept away, hissing through the water. Gripping rod with both hands I jerked with all my might. What tremendous live weight! Again—two—three—four times I struck, while my line whizzed off the reel. Hard as I jerked I never got the curved rod upright.

"You've hooked him!" yelled Captain Mitchell, with great elation. Both the boys yelled, but I could not tell what. The rush of the tuna wheeled me in the revolving chair, dragged me out of it, with knees hard on the gunwale. My rod made rapid nods. But despite the terrific strain I got the drag off. Right there began a demonstration of the efficiency of the great Coxe reel.

The tuna had run round the net, on the ocean side, and had headed toward Blue Island. I had heard the scream

[46]

of a reel, the rush of flying line, but that run beat any other I ever saw. An ordinary reel or line would have failed. Of course I had wet my line. I felt the fine spray hit my face stingingly. I could judge yards only by space on the reel, and this fish took off two hundred or more in what seemed a single flash. If he had kept on! But he ended that rush. And in two more seconds the engines were roaring and the launch was wheeling. We were after him with half my five hundred yards still on the reel.

"How about it?" shouted Sid, red-faced and fierce, bending over the open engine box.

"Slow down! Plenty of line!" I called back.

Then we got settled. The surprise of the attack had not upset us, but it had surely been electrifying. Many times on the *Gladiator*, while roaming the sea for sword-fish, had R. C. and Sid and Bob and I talked over the way to meet just such a strike and rush as this.

I sat facing the bow, rod high, line taut for several hundred feet out of the water. The tuna headed for Blue Island, about a mile away. We were leaving the dangerous labyrinth of nets. All was serene on board then.

"Some run, I'll tell the world!" rejoiced Bob. "Makes a tarpon look slow!"

I had, of course, put my drag on when the fish had slowed and we had started after him. We were running seven or eight miles an hour, and the tuna was taking line slowly off the reel. This chase extended in a straight course for some distance and it was singularly exhilarating. We all complimented the work of the little launch. The quick start was what had saved us.

"I had both engines going before you got through hooking him," boasted Sid.

When half the line had slipped off my reel I said: "Run up on him. Let me get back the line."

Sid speeded up, and I worked swiftly and hard to pump and reel, so as to recover line and not allow any slack. When I got back all that was possible at the time I was sweating and panting. Then we slowed down again.

My tuna headed up the bay and ran a mile or more before he turned. We did not want him to go up the bay, and welcomed his swerving. But when he pointed us toward the nets I was suddenly filled with dread.

"Port, Sid," I called, sharply. "Sheer off a little. We'll quarter with him and head him out to sea. . . . Or lose him right here!"

"That's the idea," replied Captain Mitchell. "Fight him now. We've got two miles before he reaches the nets."

So we ran with him yet a little to his left while I pulled with all my might and used all the drag I dared. He took line—one hundred yards—two hundred yards— three hundred yards. Still he did not turn. But he slowed down. Dragging three hundred yards of thirty-nine line, and the launch besides, told perceptibly upon his speed.

Meanwhile our other boat, with R. C. and Romer wildly waving, joined the chase, and falling in behind us kept close as possible. It was a grim ticklish time. I hated to risk so much. But that was the game—to keep him out of the nets or lose him.

"Shore he's headin' out!" yelled Bob.

That was good news, but I could not see it. Bob, however, knew more about lines in the water than I, as presently I saw proved. My tuna was slowly turning away from the dreaded nets.

"Close in, Sid. Help me get back some line," I said.

Still keeping that strain on him, we narrowed the distance between us until I had all the line back except a hundred yards or so, and with this we were well content. When we had him headed straight for the open sea we gradually moved over to a point behind him. Then I eased the drag, let him set a pace, which we adopted; and he led us out to sea. It was a great situation. The sun had come out, not bright, but enough to make the water glimmer and the distant headlands show distinctly. The lighthouse on the southwest point gradually faded; then Western Head blurred in the pale land fog; only Gull Rock and Blue Island remained in sight. We passed a bell buoy some five miles outside the bay. A foghorn bayed in faint hoarse notes its warning to mariners.

"What time did we hook up with this fellow?" I inquired.

"Seven-ten," replied Sid, consulting his watch. "It's now eight-thirty."

"Wal, I reckon it's aboot time to settle down to a fight," drawled Bob. "He's shore well hooked."

"All right. Get my coat off and put the harness on," I said.

I had never gotten much satisfaction or help out of any harness we had ever bought or made, but I expected much of the one Coxe had constructed for me. Mr. C. Alma Baker, the English angler, had liked it so well that he ordered one. It was made of leather, and like a vest with the front cut out. Straps hooked on to my rod below my reel. It felt good. I could pull with my shoulders. Thus equipped, and with gloves over thumb-stalled fingers I settled down to the grim job.

With slow steady sweeps and swift winds of reel I went through the usual procedure of fighting a heavy fish. But I could gain line only when Sid ran the boat faster than the tuna swam. Nevertheless I slowed him down in his headlong flight toward the open sea. Otherwise I could not see that I had made the slightest impression upon him. Time flies while one is fighting a fish. I was amazed when Sid sang out: "Ten-thirty—and all's well!"

There was no wind. The sea resembled a dimpled mirror. The sun shone through pale gray clouds and it was warm. The land fog began to encroach upon the sea, hiding the headlands under a silver belt. Only the dark shore line of Blue Island showed us the direction of the bay.

We were eight miles off before I stopped the tuna and turned him. I was not in the best of condition for a hard, grueling battle, as I had fought only one fish during the summer—a 413-pound broadbill swordfish. I had tried to keep fit, but there is nothing like actual work with a rod on a fish to keep an angler hard and strong.

At the end of three hours I was wet and hot. All this time, even when I had pulled my hardest, the tuna had continued to tow the launch. Sometimes more slowly than at others, but always he towed it, bow first! Most of this strain had fallen upon my back and shoulders, where the harness fitted so snugly. And about this time I made the discovery that, if I held high on the rod and let all the strain come on it instead of the harness, I could stand the mighty pull for only about two minutes at a stretch. Then I would have to transfer the strain back to the harness. Which of course meant to my shoulders! I felt chafed under the arms and I ached a little, but otherwise did not appear to be suffering any great discomfort from this unusual demand on my muscles. It struck me forcibly, however, that the tuna was towing the launch absolutely by pulling against my back. What amazed me was the great value of the Coxe harness. During all this time, which seemed short, the fight itself

MARKET FISHERMEN NETTING TUNA

PLATE IX

ROMER FISHING WITH THE BOYS FOR SCULPIN

PLATE X

and the remarks of my comrades, especially the droll speech of my Florida boatman Bob, kept me in a state of excitement. Probably I could not have felt even an injury at that stage.

All fights with big fish have stages, and this one was no exception. The great tuna came to the surface, and abandoning a straight course out to sea he began to swim in circles. He was still fast, still strong. But he had shown his first indication of weakening. He had lost sense of direction. He was bewildered. He pushed a wave ahead of him and left a wide wake behind.

"Bob, get up on the bow and watch him," I ordered. "Never take your eye off him!"

An experienced fisherman such as Bob, if he could see a fish, could tell exactly what he was going to do. It turned out that I had chosen wisely to give this scout duty to Bob. The tuna was in front a couple of hundred feet and half as far to starboard. He was deep under the surface, so that I could see only the waves he started in motion. But to Bob he was visible. Suddenly he shouted, piercingly: "Look out!"

I saw a surge in the water and a pale gleam, incredibly swift, right at the boat. Leaping up, I threw off the drag and plunged my rod deep in the water. Not a second too soon! All I saw was the bag of line shoot under the boat. Then I felt a lunge on my rod, and the whir of the reel. Sid had been as swift with levers and wheel. Bob and Captain Mitchell were leaning over the gunwale.

"All clear!" sang out Sid.

"Son-of-a-gun!" ejaculated Bob. "Talk about puttin' it in high!"

"Splendid work!" declared Captain Mitchell, rising. "By jove! but he made a dash!"

I lifted the dripping rod and reel, fell back in the seat,

jammed the butt in the socket, and tightening the drag I faced about to look for the tuna. What a cunning wonderful rush that had been! If Bob had not been standing on the bow I would never have perceived that action in time to avert disaster. A bagged line floating on the surface and dragged under a boat oftener than not will cut off on the propeller. It had been a narrow shave.

"Boys, we've got to get mad or he'll fool us, same as that one did yesterday," I said.

We all grew silent and watchful then. I began to conserve strength, to leave more to my reel, to study every move of the tuna, to make absolutely sure he never had an inch of slack line. As he circled here and there at random, sometimes in wide curves, at others in short turns, he always towed the launch. I kept on a good stiff drag, but not strong enough to break the line, should he suddenly rush. And the line paid off the reel slowly as he dragged the launch. Sid said he towed us four miles an hour, but I thought that a little too much. But he kept us moving. Gradually he drew us back toward the bell buoy, and round this he hung, near or far, as it happened. During this strenuous hour he never sounded once. Always that bulge on the smooth surface and the swelling wake behind! These were new and fascinating tactics in a game fish.

About at this period of the battle the physical man began to rebel. There is a limit to the time emotion and imagination can make a man oblivious to pain and fatigue. Long had I been tired, but it was a tired feeling I rather reveled in. It had not made any difference. But suddenly I was made to realize that something was wrong. My hands, wrists, arms were still strong, and I felt that I had reserve in them for what we call the finish of a fight, sometimes the most strenuous part. My shoulders likewise seemed as good as ever. But my back, low down where the harness fit so like a glove, had begun to hurt. I thought about this carefully. We never mind pangs. It would not be any achievement to catch a great fish without toil and sweat, endurance and pain. Anybody can catch some kind of a fish without these. But no one will ever catch a great tuna without them. Accidents happen, and the lucky-fluke captures of giant game fish are on record. But I never had one and I do not take any account of them. So up to that point I had not paid any particular attention to my growing discomforts. I decided the pain in my back was due to a different kind of pull. In fact, my whole body was pulled. It was harnessed to that tuna. But I could stand the strain, and so entered upon the second half of the struggle.

The weather grew even better, if that were possible. The sea appeared flat without heave or swell. Not a breath of wind stirred. The transparent film of cloud let sunlight through, but little heat. It seemed a wonderfully lucky day.

R. C. and Romer in the large boat followed us, plying cameras and motion-picture machines with great assiduity. Sometimes they came within a hundred feet behind us or off to one side. I could hear the boy's shrill voice: "Some fish! Hang on, dad! You can lick him! Don't work too hard! Let him pull the boat!" Occasionally R. C. yelled a word of encouragement. I waved to them once in a while until the time came when I forgot everything but the tuna.

While I went through the labored motions with rod and reel I waited and hoped for some expression from Bob that we had a chance to whip this fish. Bob knew fish nature as well as Sid knew the workings of an engine. And I knew I could absolutely rely on what Bob said. But what a long time I waited! He stood balanced on the bow, his keen profile against the sky, his eyes glued to the shadowy blue shape of the tuna.

"Wal," he said, finally, "if the hook doesn't tear out we'll lick him."

That gave me renewed life and energy.

"If he ever heads this way yell to me, so I can release the strain," I replied. "We just won't pull the hook out."

Captain Mitchell sat or stood at my side all the while, sometimes silent, often giving a quiet word of praise or encouragement. He was always optimistic. "You're going to kill this tuna," he averred. "I'm a lucky man to have in the boat." He was particularly keen to observe our handling of the launch and manipulation of tackle; and it was plain he was deeply and favorably impressed.

"We always have a long double line above the leader," he said. "Then when we get the end of that over the reel we hold hard and let the tuna tow the skiff around. When it's safe to do so we have the boatmen row against the fish."

"But, Captain, wouldn't a tuna like this one tow a skiff all day and all night?" I queried.

"I'm afraid so. He's a mighty game fish and a big one. Some tuna give up quicker than others. One now and then is a terrific and unbeatable fighter. This fellow amazes me. He's a stubborn devil."

I had an eighteen-foot leader and double line about the same length. It was an occasion for cheers when I got the end of the double line up to the tip of my rod the first time. But I could not get it over the reel. After several more attempts and aided by Sid slipping in closer on the fish, I did get the double line over my reel. That was a signal victory which we all celebrated. Also we saw the end of the leader. These things marked another stage in the fight—hopeful ones for me. I had most trouble in going slow, in holding back, in maintaining patience. It must necessarily be a very long contest. But to know this and to practice it were vastly different things. The sweat from my forehead ran down in my eyes and over my nose.

To and fro over the unruffled ocean we glided, seldom under our own power. Now and then Sid would throw in the clutch of one engine to help me get back some line. Bob stuck to his post on the bow and had nothing to say. Captain Mitchell did not let me grow discouraged.

"He's shoving a bigger wave all the time," he said. "That means he's swimming higher. Soon his fins and tail will show."

Sure enough they did. His ragged dorsal, and the long curved yellow spike behind it, and then his blue-black tail, at last cut the calm surface of the water. Yells from the other boat attested to the close attention and pursuit our comrades were giving us. During the next half hour we sighted his fins many times, always within a hundred feet. I could have held him at that distance just as long as my strength would stand it, but when we got him close so he saw the boat he would move ahead. A hundred times more or less we ran him down and I dragged him within thirty feet of where Bob stood. Gradually he got used to the boat and always he tired almost imperceptibly. All I could see was the last third of his body, the huge taper of his blue bulk, decorated with the little yellow rudderlike fins, and his wagging tail. But of course Bob could see every inch of him. At length I had to yell:

"Say, Bob, how big is he?"

"Huh! I'm shore afraid to say," replied Bob.

"Tell me!"

"Wal, it'll do you more good not to know."

"Where's he—hooked?" I panted.

[55]

"Deep, I reckon. I see the leader comin' out of his mouth on this side."

"Is he wearing out?"

"He can't put it in high any more, that's shore. Just hang on an' save yourself for the finish."

"But I won't—have—much to save."

Time and again the tuna got the leader round his tail. This made the rod wag up and down in a kind of weaving motion, and it lifted me to and fro in my chair. So far as we could see, it did not inconvenience the tuna in the least. When a Marlin or broadbill gets tangled in the leader, he cannot fight until it is free again. But not so with this tuna!

"Sid, ease in behind him," I called. "I'm going to pull the leader up to Bob. Captain, you go forward and get ready for a possible chance to gaff him."

"Not yet! It's too soon," replied Captain Mitchell.

"It may not come soon. But I want you there. . . . Bob, grab the leader and hold it—not stiff—but just enough to let it slip. We'll see. Now, all do as I say—and if we lose him I'll be to blame."

I shut down on the drag and began to haul and wind with all I had left. Of course, without Sid's help I never could have pumped the leader out of the water, not at that time. No man unaided could have pulled that tuna toward him. In a few moments Bob's eager sinewy hands closed on the end of the leader just below the ring. He never uttered a word, but I saw his tense expression change. The others whooped. That relieved me of the terrific strain. It was such a change that for an instant my head swam.

The tuna did not like it. He lashed the water white. He towed us faster. Then he pulled the leader away from Bob.

"Boys, we'll try that," I said, doggedly. "We'll keep

at him. Be quick, careful. Do the right thing at the right time."

"Reckon it's our chance," replied Bob. "I'll shore handle that leader easy. It'll work if the hook doesn't tear out."

Then I had the task of hauling that leader back to Bob. It took moments of strenuous work. Bob stood far out on the bow, reaching for it. The double line passed him. It would have been risky at that stage to have trusted to the double line. When he got hold of the leader I had another little rest. What welcome relief! I was burning, throbbing, aching. Still both hands and arms were strong. I felt that I could last it out. The tuna lashed the water and sheered to starboard. Sid had one engine in reverse, the other full speed ahead, and he was working the wheel. Quick as we turned, however, we could not keep the leader from being torn out of Bob's hands. The tuna made a roar on the surface and sounded. He went to the bottom. I had the pleasant job of lifting him. As a matter of fact I did not budge him an inch. But I pulled as mightily as I could and persuaded him to come up again. Then we went after him. I got the leader to Bob, and once more was free of that awful drag at my vitals. Bob held the fish rather longer this time, and Sid threw out the clutches.

We warmed to these tactics, for in them we saw sure capture of the tuna, if the tackle held. My task seemed tremendous. When the tuna sheered away, tearing the leader from Bob, I had to haul it back. I could turn the fish now and move him a very little. But oh, what a ponderous weight! When he shook his head I thought he would crack my back. Many times we tried this, so many that after fifteen I quit counting them. But they worked. The tuna was weakening. If I did not give out first we might get him. Every time now I could see him, and the sight seemed to inspire me momentarily with the strength of Hercules. It was that sight of him, marvelous blue massive body and tail, and the short rest following my getting the leader to Bob, which kept me up.

After what seemed a long while Bob was able to hold to the leader while the tuna towed us round and round. Then began another stage, that of hauling him closer. At first it would not work. When Bob hauled away hand over hand, very cautiously and slowly for a few feet, then the tuna would lunge and break away. By degrees, however, this method worked as had the mere holding of the leader. The awful thing for me was that now when the fish tore the leader out of Bob's hands he would sound and I had to pump him up. There was nothing else to do. I had to do it. Both my excitement and agony augmented, yet somehow I was able to carry on and keep a cool head.

When Bob finally turned to us with his keen blue eyes flashing I knew something was up.

"I can hold the leader an' drag him. If we all work right now he's marchin' to his funeral."

How cool he was! I knew he lent us all confidence. Sid had surely had his hands full at the wheel and clutches. I was worn to a frazzle. But Bob's patience and endurance seemed to grow. He looked at me.

"A few more times an' he's a lost fawn-skin," he said, tersely. "Don't let him rest. Haul him up to me."

"Bob—your—words—sound—like music," I panted. "Sure—I'll haul him—right up."

My tuna was down deep. He had become almost a dead weight. Yet every wag of head or tail had irresistible power. Fortunately his wags had become few. I had now to favor my lame back. I pulled with my arms, lifted with my knees. Only such a tackle as this could

Six-Hundred-and-Eighty-Four-Pound Tuna (Plates xi to xiv)

PLATE XI

PLATE XII

PLATE XIII

PLATE XIV

ever have lifted this fish. I was afraid something would break. But reel, rod, line, all held. At last I heaved him out of the depths. When Bob got the leader again I gasped.

"Hang on—till I come to!"

Then Bob began what turned out to be the greatest performance I had ever seen. He held the tuna. Sometimes he would let a yard or two of the leader slip through his hands, to relieve the strain of a roll or lunge, but he never let go of it. He was pulled from side to side as the fish wagged across the bow; sometimes on his knees; again straddling the leader; often bent forward almost ready to let go. His face was sharp and stern and full of tense cords of pain. It must have hurt to hold that wire. Sid's motions were no less active and tense. According to Bob's signs, which came mostly through nods of his head, Sid had to throw the clutches in or out, reverse one and full speed ahead on the other, all the time working the wheel. The launch spun like a top; it never went straight any more. How the two of them kept that tuna from running under the boat was astounding to see. But they accomplished it. I was on edge, however, ready at a second's notice to act my part and plunge the rod overboard to save the line from fouling on the propellers. I had also to keep the line from catching on the bow or the gaff in Mitchell's hands, and as much as possible out of Bob's way. This strain was almost as hard to bear as had been the one of weight.

Thus the fight narrowed down to the climax. Many times the huge tuna rolled within reach of the long gaff. But I wanted a sure chance. Bob knew when far better than I, and he never said a word. Captain Mitchell leaned over one gunwale, then the other. Sid had begun to wear nervous under the strain. He talked a good deal, mostly to himself. He had many things to operate all at once, and to do so without mistake required tremendous concentration. Back and forth he swiftly bent from wheel to clutches.

The tuna heaved on the surface, he rolled and gasped, lunged out his huge head with jaws wide and black eyes staring—a paralyzing sight for me. Then he wagged toward the bow, his wide back round and large as a barrel, out of the water.

"Gaff him!" I yelled, hoarsely.

Captain Mitchell reached over him and hauled on the big gaff. It did not even stick in the fish for a second. I could not speak. I expected the tuna to smash our boat and break away. But he only rolled wearily, and Bob dragged him closer. Captain Mitchell tried again with like result. I feared he did not know how to use a detachable gaff such as we had built for swordfish. I yelled for Sid to try. He leaped over the engine box, attached the gaff to the pole, and extended it out. The tuna was rolling alarmingly. My heart stopped beating.

"Take time. He's all in," shouted Bob, cool and hard.

Sid dropped the wide hook over the broad back and lunged back with all his might. He pulled the tuna against the launch. Bang! Slap! The big tail jarred me almost off my feet.

"Shiver our timbers!" yelled Bob. "That gaff won't go in his body. It's too big."

Sid hauled the gaff in, and plunging over the gunwale he caught the fish on the side of the head. It did not go deep, but it held. Still if the tuna had been capable of violent action he would have torn away. Captain Mitchell as quickly put the other gaff in the mouth of the fish and jerked it through his jaw. Then Bob followed that action with a rope, slipping it through the ring on the gaff. When I saw the great fish had finally and surely been captured I flopped back in my chair, dizzy, reeling, scarcely aware of the acclaim about my ears.

We towed him back to the bay and up to the lighthouse. In lieu of a flag we flew a red kite, by way of celebration. My aches seemed strangely trivial.

It took five men to haul that tuna out on the bank. I shall not soon forget the eyes of my son Romer, or his wild whirling words, when he saw my tuna close at hand. R. C. stood in mute admiration. Sid and Bob were more elated than I had ever seen them. The native fishermen marveled at such a catch on a rod and line. Captain Mitchell radiated delight and congratulations.

"Gamest tuna I ever saw or heard of!" was his praise of the fish.

He measured 8 feet 4 inches in length, 6 feet 2 inches in girth, and weighed 684 pounds.

It took me a long time to realize the actual fact of his capture. But by gloating over him and photographing him and hanging around him I at last arrived at some sane appreciation of his tremendous bulk and remarkable beauty.

He was built like a colossal steel projectile, with a deep dark blue color on the back, shading to an exquisite abalone opal hue toward the under side, which was silver white. He blazed like the shield of Achilles. From the edge of his gill cover to the tip of his nose was two feet. He had eyes as large as saucers. His gaping mouth was huge enough to take in a bucket. His teeth were like a strip of sand paper, very fine and small. The massive roundness of his head, the hugeness of his body, fascinated me and made me marvel at the speed he had been capable of. What incalculable power in that wide tail! I had to back away to several rods' distance before I could appreciate the full immensity of him.

Then when the men hung him up! I could not believe my eyes. He seemed another and a vaster fish, with a beautiful broadness, depth, fullness, all that signified the wonder of his growth and the mysterious power of the sea that had nourished him.

The fine weather did not last long. About four o'clock the sky darkened over and a wind from the east brought scudding gray clouds and a fine rain. The native fishermen predicted a northeaster. By five o'clock wind and rain had increased and before dark we were storm-beaten. R. C. and I had our beds in the launch, his on a cot and mine on the floor. We expected the canvas hood to protect us. It might have served for an ordinary rain, but not for the deluge that descended upon us. It roared on the canvas and leaked through. The bilge filled rapidly. We could hear the water splashing. I was too tired and full of aches to care what happened. The boys were very solicitous and said I would drown if I stayed on the floor of the launch. But I went to sleep in the midst of the storm and did not awaken until I was rested, some time in the early morning hours. The storm had slackened, yet the rain still fell, in drizzles and gusts. I could hear the boom of the surf on the island out in the bay, and the hoarse bellow of the fog-horn. My bed was wet outside, but warm and dry within, and I enjoyed the sound of the elements.

Morning brought lowering fog and drab, somber surroundings and more rain. We were hard put to it to pass the time. Bob, however, had a task to skin the big tuna for mounting. At intervals the rain ceased. We saw tuna out in the bay, and during the afternoon tried to get a bite out of one. Captain Mitchell and R. C. saw a much larger tuna than mine. He passed directly under the boat. They estimated his weight at over a thousand pounds. But though tuna appeared plentiful, they were not feeding. Then the fog and rain rolled in again, blanketing us for another uncomfortable night. It rained all night.

Next morning the storm was gone, the wind had veered, and there were indications of clearing weather. At six o'clock we started down the bay, very glad for a little pale sunshine. A heavy swell was running. Great white breakers dashed up on the rocky shores.

When we got to the fishing grounds we found the fishermen at their nets, evidently unconcerned about the heavy sea. The swells were mountainous. The first fisherman we accosted said there had been a tuna at his net a little while before. We bought a bushel of herring and set about fishing, with R. C. at the rod.

Soon another fisherman hailed us. We ran over to his boat and saw the huge swirl of a tuna on the surface. I was thrilled with the certainty that R. C. would soon get a strike. Several times this fish swirled on the surface. Captain Mitchell saw him pass near our boat. But nothing happened there, and soon another fisherman called us over to try for a tuna round his net.

"Only a few round this morning and they're not hungry," he said. "They'll take a couple of herring, then leave. Yesterday morning we saw a good many."

Later two other of the herring fishermen beckoned for us, and when we hastened to them informed us there was a tuna there. We saw one swirl. But we could not get a bite for R. C. The sea grew rough and we decided we could not very well fight a fish if we did not hook one, so we returned to the breakwater.

I took advantage of the opportunity to drive back to Liverpool for mail, supplies, and to send telegrams relative to my lucky catch.

The driver carried me over another road, part of which led through what was called Nine-Mile Woods. After the heavy rains the wild country appeared intersected by running streams. It was a moose country, green and flat in places, meadows alternating with heavy spruce forest, and in some places very rough and rocky. The streams were beautiful. Gold-brown water swirled and glided out of the dark wet woods. Spots of white foam floated along; waterfalls roared and foamed; still black pools gleamed under the dense foliage; white flowers bordered the brooks; ferns and grasses waved in the edge of the current. Big gray boulders, amber with moss, broke the level monotony. Spruce trees, maples, ash, pine, lined the narrow wet road. Arbor vitæ and huckleberry bushes spread thicker covering over the open patches. How green, cool, wet, mossy, fresh with rain and sparkling with dewdrops! It was a country used to water. The verdure grew heavy, thick, dark. What a contrast to the desert! I bathed my eyes in a soothing balm of nature. After the red and yellow wastes of Arizona, and the glaring openness of the Pacific, where I had spent the last three months, this green and verdant northland was most satisfying and welcome.

The driver of the car told me an interesting thing, which later I verified. Several years ago Mr. Whitney broke off a tuna. The following summer this same fish was caught in a net and was identified by the leader and hook still attached. This seems a remarkable circumstance. I am inclined to believe it singularly unusual. Most fish that get away with hooks in their gullets become prey for sharks or die. These giant tuna, however, might present an exception to this rule. They are so tremendously big, virile, and powerful that it takes more to affect them than in the case of ordinary tuna or other fish. I have not seen a shark in these waters, though the fishermen say there are a few here. Most probably this icy water, straight from the Arctic seas, is too cold for the warm-water shark. The temperature is about fifty degrees. It is a beautifully clear green water, not like the blue of the Pacific. It makes me think of glistening green-white icebergs, and most assuredly it feels as if it had lately been closely associated with them.

Upon my return to East Jordon, wind and sea had fallen and the sun shone warm. It was an afternoon to bask in the warmth on the breakwater, drying blankets, clothes, cameras, fishing lines, and everything else that was wet. Not a tuna had been seen during the day, though a close watch was kept. The fishermen seemed to have an idea that both herring and albacore were leaving the bay. They had been here in abundance for five weeks. Nevertheless we had great hopes of raising one for R. C. on the morrow, and made preparations to get up at four o'clock.

Toward morning the air grew frosty. I was awake on and off, and by four o'clock, which was the hour for arising, I felt quite ready to crawl out. R. C. was slow. I heard Bob say: "Wal, when it gets to makin' frost it's time for me to stick a feather in my hat an' beat it for home."

The moon was a pale bright silver, and the sky a steely cold blue. The morning star burned with the same hue. Indeed it was the northland. A soft pearly-gray fog hovered over bay and forest; and the wild fringed horizon seemed unfamiliar and strange to me. While I took some brisk exercise along the breakwater the east brightened and presently it was daylight. Still there was no color anywhere. All pale gray, somber, cold tones! We had breakfast, and were gliding down the bay before five o'clock.

Gradually the pale east took fire and glowed, the

clouds changing, until the sun rose, golden red, throwing a glimmering track upon the water. I saw the lighthouse on the headland to the south, and it blinked like a great star. Gull Rock and Blue Island appeared begirt by white surges, and a dull steady roar came from shore.

Four boats bobbed upon the water. The first fisher-man we approached said he had seen a tuna about day-light. We bought a barrel of bait from him, and were soon ready. Two near-by fishermen beckoned to us, and we ran over to where they were hauling their net. One of them threw out a herring and pointed. Immediately I saw a huge boiling bulge on the water. I yelled, and at once excitement claimed us. We fastened to their buoy. R. C. threw out his bait and Captain Mitchell threw out herring. I was standing high on the bow.

Suddenly a shield-shaped blaze of silver-green flashed through the water. It came from a great tuna. He took the loose herring and made a heavy break on the surface. All of us except R. C. were shouting at the same time. The next herring Captain Mitchell threw out did not sink. A huge shadow loomed out of the green water. Smash! The tuna lunged on the surface. I saw his broad blue back, his fins, his tail. He missed the herring. His quick movement amazed me. He was as fast as a trout. Next time he got the herring, leaving a swirling eddy behind. But for me, this time, the light was bad and I could not see him. We expected him to take R. C.'s bait, but he so plainly avoided it that we made certain he was a cautious tuna. Captain Mitchell kept throwing out herring and the great fish kept rising out of the green depths to take them. It was as exasperating as it was thrilling. Once he flashed by broadside to us, only a few yards away and a few feet under the surface. I saw every line of him, clear-cut, green and gold. He was enormous. His big black eye showed distinctly. I saw

him open his mouth wide and gulp the herring. He
closed his jaw and swept away. The whole motion
seemed just one flash. How perfectly incredible!

He took every herring we threw out, except the one
on R. C.'s line. Finally Captain Mitchell threw out
R. C.'s bait and another herring at the same moment.
Both sank slowly. Then—up flashed the monster, swift
as light. He made a mistake in his choice of the two
herring. He got R. C.'s hook. The line swept out and
R. C. lunged back on the rod.

I turned to throw off the buoy. Sid jammed at the
self-starters. In a second we were moving. That fish
cleared the net and headed inshore, going like a bullet.
We followed at top speed, the water flying from our
bows. Still he took line. When we had two hundred
yards off the reel the strain slackened. We thought he
had fouled the line on a buoy rope and broken off. But
it turned out he had wheeled back on us, gaining slack
line, and the hook had come out. We were pretty hard
hit, but went back hopefully to try over again.

Another fisherman signaled us. Before we reached
him we saw a boil on the water near his net, and that
revived all the thrilling sensations. Here we employed
the same tactics. The second time R. C.'s bait was
thrown out the tuna came up for it. I could not see
well. But Captain Mitchell saw it. R. C. jerked with
all his might. There was a screech from the reel—then
the hook pulled loose. More bad luck! It seemed to
hurt me more than any of the others.

"You tried to hook him too soon," I argued. "Let him
have a little line."

Bob backed me up in this. Captain Mitchell said he
never let tuna have any line, especially when only one
was working round the boat. But with all due respect
to the Captain's practice I insisted that R. C. give the

next fish a chance to move away with the bait. R. C. said this was what he had wanted to do in the first place, but our differing suggestions had upset him.

"Three bites!" I ejaculated, incredulously. I could not realize it, and perhaps I felt all the more because of the actuality of it.

Then my roving eye caught sight of a fisherman waving to us, some two hundred yards away. We were quick to run his way. Long before we got near I saw an enormous splash, right under his gunwale. The water flew over the boat. The fisherman threw out another herring. Smash! The tuna had it.

We soon tied on to the buoy, and as the fisherman's boat drifted off we began to chum, throw in herring, and let out R. C.'s bait in the midst of it. This tuna rose like a bass to take a grasshopper on the surface. *Wop!* His mouth opened and sucked in the herring, and a cloud of silver scales floated away in the green water. We were all on the *qui vive* for another bite, and surely expected it. I stood on the bow, heedless of the launch rising on the huge swells, and watched with strained eyes. The sun had come out brighter, so that I had a much better chance to see under the surface. Again Captain Mitchell threw out a herring.

"There he comes!" I yelled. "Oh! did you see him take it?"

"Did we?" they all answered together, and even R. C. joined it. His eyes were sticking out. No wonder! Of all the fish sights I had ever seen, this one was the greatest. Blue, silver, green, gold—how the colors shone! The ponderous grace of the fish, the gliding action, the single wave of his forked tail, the little fringe of yellow rudders, the savage gap of his mouth as he seized the herring, the turn and the flash—these features I seemed to take in all in a glance. Then he was gone. But he arose again to the next herring. Again and again he took loose bait. But he would not take R. C.'s. He moved the leader as he swept by it. And we fed him herring, one after another, marveling at the magnificent sight of him flashing in the sunlight, sheering down to vanish, until he would not rise any more. Then we chummed for a while.

All the boats except one had left the fishing grounds. This was Saturday, and preparatory to Sunday the fishermen took up their nets and left. The one man left had shown us more than one favor, and I kept watch on him hopefully. Suddenly I espied him raise a piece of canvas and wave it. The distance was far and some of the boys thought I had made a mistake. But I knew I was right, and soon we were flying back up the bay toward this last boat. A mass of floating sea grass surrounded him. Before we reached him I saw boils on the surface.

"Hey! they're here—a lot of them!" he called, as we drew near.

We were soon in position, as before, except that Bob held to the stern of the fisherman's boat. R. C. threw over his bait, and Captain Mitchell stood with herring poised, ready to cast it. But he never did. I saw a green shadow come out from under our boat. I would have yelled wildly if I had not been paralyzed. The beautiful fish showed every line, every spot and feature. He moved easily, opened his mouth, took in the bait, closed his jaws on it, and glided on, flashed, gleamed, faded, vanished. R. C. let him take line off the reel—ten —twenty—thirty feet. Then he shut down on the drag and struck mightily. What a lunge! R. C. was lifted out of his seat. I whirled to throw off the buoy. It got tangled on our line and I took some valuable seconds releasing it.

[69]

Sid and Bob were yelling. I heard the engines roaring. But we were not moving right. Too slow! And R. C.'s line was whizzing off the reel. I did not know what was wrong, but something was.

"Quick there! Get after him!" I yelled.

"Doing our best," yelled back Sid. "Propellers caught in sea grass."

R. C.'s line went out with a rapidity that appalled me. Three hundred yards—four hundred! When only a little line was left and I was about ready to succumb the propellers cut loose from the sea grass, and we shot ahead so swiftly that all of us except R. C., who was sitting down, were thrown off our balance. I fell off the bow. Wonder indeed that I fell into the boat instead of out of it! When I recovered my equilibrium the boys and Captain Mitchell were shouting at the top of their lungs. R. C.'s face was a sight to behold! All of us had given up that tuna and line. I leaped back on the bow.

We were now running almost at full speed and it was hard to stand up there. I grasped the bow rope with my left hand and rose to my feet. We could not gain an inch on the fish. The line was stretched like a banjo string, and as it cut the water it picked up strands of sea grass. Bob leaned over and tore this grass off, and as fast as another bunch collected he removed that also.

"He's shore got it in high!" he yelled.

This run discounted any other I had ever seen. Straight up the bay the tuna led us a mile—fully three miles—then inshore another mile, before we began to gain on him.

"If he doesn't break off, that run will kill him!" shouted Bob.

R. C. looked both rapt and grim.

I saw that there were still fifty or more yards on his reel, and I was not worried now. We were holding our own. How the rod nodded and the line sang! R. C. began to try to recover line. He hauled far back, and swinging forward tried to wind the reel. In vain! He could not get an inch.

"Sid, have you any more speed?" I called.

"A little. But we're going like h—— now. I'm afraid I can't stop her quick enough," he replied.

"We'll take a chance."

Then the chase was truly wonderful. Our motor launch, with two engines at full speed, roared across the bay, leaving a huge V-shaped wake. We had outrun our other boat. This accelerated speed soon brought the desired results. R. C. began to recover line. Gradually he worked half of it back, and then just when we began to feel safe again the tuna ended that extraordinary run. Sid slowed up. R. C. pumped and reeled like a swift machine. Soon with four hundred yards back on the reel we burst into acclaims, each in his own particular feeling for the moment.

"That run would kill any fish," called Bob, quick and sharp. "R. C., you hand it to him for all you're worth, before he gets his wind! I tell you—shore as you're born he's a lost fawn-skin."

He was so electrifying in his keen spirit and assurance that R. C. set to work with might and main, exerting himself to the utmost, saving nothing. My task was to watch the line, to make sure which way the tuna turned. As I was high up I could see fully fifty feet of the line after it entered the water. He was swimming high. Often I would look back to get a glimpse of R. C. He never varied that tremendous winchlike action of shoulders and that whirl of the reel. He was red-faced and sweating, with the white shadows showing under his eyes, always a mark of great exertion in him. The engines were running, but the clutches were out. R. C. and the tuna

[71]

together made the launch sail through the water. The moments seemed as nothing.

Four times R. C. got the double line over the reel, only to lose it. The fifth time he held it and gained more. Then I saw the tuna. He was laboring, fighting that tremendous strain. He had not yet gotten his wind.

Suddenly I discerned a green-white wavering shape. I feared more keenly. The tuna was swimming on his side.

"Work hard!" I burst out. "He's coming!"

Foot by foot the double line slipped by me. At last I saw the leader. Then the fish turned farther on his side. R. C. was dragging him. The launch was slipping closer. There! I saw him clear. He gaped. He rolled. Oh—fish of fishes!

"Just what I said!" yelled Bob, leaping up beside me. And in a second more he had the leader.

I picked up the small gaff and turned, finding something of coolness at the finish.

"Steady, R. C. Look for a rush! . . . Sid, throw her out and grab a gaff."

When I faced forward again the tuna was rolling and gasping on the surface, just under the bow, a terrifying and magnificent sight.

I fell down and leaned over with the gaff. What would happen to me? I reached for him.

"Careful! Quick! In the mouth!" called Bob's keen voice in my ears. He was kneeling over me. Quickly I slipped the gaff into the wide-open jaws and jerked hard. The tuna wagged his head. What an awful wrench he gave my arms! I thought they would be torn out by the roots. My feet went high in the air. Bob's powerful hand clutched my shirt. I did not go overboard nor release the gaff. Then Sid plunged the big swordfish gaff into the tuna.

[72]

For a little while then all was roar and splash and straining arms. It took the three of us to hold him. But at last he was overcome. Then with a rope round his tail we fell back into the launch to gaze amazedly at each other.

"Once in my life I had some good luck!" ejaculated R. C. "Another half hour of that and he would have cracked my spine!"

We towed him up the bay, having only a mile to go to the breakwater. He had been hooked seven miles down the bay. Many and various were the remarks made by us upon that triumphant procession. Not one of us had remembered to take note of the time he was hooked. But the whole performance fell short of an hour. Bob had been right. That terrific run had taken his strength for the time being.

"All mackerel are alike," declared Bob. "A long run takes their wind."

This is true of Pacific tuna, and seemed to have been so in the case of R. C.'s tuna. But I was inclined to say that a combination of this remarkable run and R. C.'s Herculean exertion had accounted for the unparalleled record time for a fight with such a fish.

We hauled him out on the grass—a spectacle for anglers. Length, 8 feet 7 inches. Girth, 5 feet 10 inches. He was therefore a longer slimmer fish than mine. But the bulk of him, hung up, looked vastly otherwise than slim. He weighed 638 pounds.

The afternoon passed swiftly enough, with photographing R. C.'s fish, care of tackle and launch, and talking about the performance of the several tuna we had hooked.

The wind died away early and there was a promise of an unusual sunset. It turned out to be strikingly beautiful. Scattered clouds to north and west quickly changed from white to gold, and then to rose. As I had noted before, the color was exquisitely fresh and vivid, and magnified by reflection in the water. I sat beneath the old deserted lighthouse and tried to absorb the beauty and glory of it all. The water changed even more vividly than the clouds, and when the sun sank to give place to the afterglow there was no adequate expression for the blaze and the shimmer of the bay. There were spaces of purple and violet, dark as the sky at midnight, and supremely mysterious with shadows and depths. Northward where high amber clouds shone lustrously the reflection on the water resembled myriads of quivering jewels, such as opal and topaz. To the south the bay seemed a rippling lake of rose, delicate and dark, conforming strangely to hue and line of clouds. This colorful pageant lasted a long time, only very gradually losing its brilliance, and dying at length into the cold clear northern twilight.

During the night the wind veered to its old quarter, the southeast, and it brought back the fog and the rain. Some little boys visited us and I noted that they had on rubber boots and slickers. I asked them if they wore these to school and they answered in the affirmative. It gave me an inspiration.

We left the boats and motored back to Liverpool, where we purchased rubber boots, coats, pants, and hats called southwesters. Now let it rain!

Reports as to fish around Liverpool were not encouraging. But few herring had been brought in, and no tuna had been seen. The main body of herring, the second run, had not yet begun. We spent Sunday motoring inland to Annapolis, to see a three-masted schooner that I contemplated purchasing, and returned late at night.

Next morning a pall of dark cloud and rain had set-

R. C.'s First Great Tuna (Plates xv to xviii)

PLATE XV

PLATE XVI

PLATE XVII

PLATE XVIII

tled down, as if to discourage us for good. But we went on with our plans just the same. The ride back to East Jordon was made through teeming rain and over flooded roads. About four o'clock the storm let up, and there seemed some indication of a shift in the wind.

Schools of tuna had been seen in the bay on Saturday afternoon, and none since. The herring had become scarce. I rowed the skiff round for an hour, trying to keep warm. Upon my return to the boats I observed the men loading a half dozen cans of gasoline from the wharf to the deck of the larger boat. I thought at the moment some of the cans might slip overboard. Our small launch was moored next to the large boat. The canvas hood was up. Bob was tinkering around the engines. Sid, all bundled up in heavy clothes, and with his rubber things on over them, was moving about on the deck. I tied the skiff to one of the piles. Suddenly a heavy sodden splash alarmed me.

"There goes our gasoline!" I shouted as I looked up.

The launch appeared to be righting itself from a violent lurch. Bob was bending over, performing some unusual gymnastics.

"Save the funnel! Save the funnel!" he yelled to somebody.

Then I was certain the cans of gasoline had fallen overboard. But further heavy splashing between the boats added curiosity to my alarm.

"Say, Bob, what on earth's happened?"

"Nothin'. Sid just fell in!" he replied.

Then a sputtering gasping voice followed: "Can't swim. . . . Help me—out!"

Whereupon I got out of the skiff and ran along the wharf, in time to see Captain Pence haul Sid out of the water into the boat. Bundled up as he was, he afforded a spectacle calculated to excite mirth in anyone. I had to sit down.

"Where have you—been—Sid?" I asked.

"—— —— fell in!" he choked, indignantly. "Bob's fault. When I jumped on to the launch—he must have done somethin'. Because she careened over. I couldn't hold on. I fell in. And I sank like lead. Thought I'd drown sure, before I could kick up. . . . Then that darned Florida mullet-fisherman yelled, 'Save the funnel!' . . . When I was drownin'. . . . Oh, boy, it was cold! We don't know what ice water is in California."

"Save the funnel!" I echoed. "By golly! that's immense!" And I had the heartiest laugh for many a long day.

Rain and fog soon drove me to shelter under the awning of the launch, where, snug in the blankets, I was soon asleep. I awoke at different times during the night. The rain had ceased. Morning disclosed a northwest wind and a promise of clearing weather. At five-thirty we were on our way to the fishing grounds. Blue sky showed in the west, and the east lightened. I saw to my satisfaction that a good day was at hand.

But we did not find any net fishermen out between Gull Rock and Blue Island. There were no nets set. Finally inshore beyond Gull Rock we saw some boats and we ran in on them, to find several fishermen making for home. They had only a few herring. Reported the fish very scarce.

We ran inshore with them, where we bought a couple of bushels of bait, in fact all that had been caught that morning. One of the fishermen said there had been tuna round his net that morning. We ran back. Meanwhile the sun had come out bright and warm and the sea was rippling and sparkling.

R. C., who was on the big boat, had seen a tuna during our absence. We picked up one of the net-buoys and began to chum right there. But no tuna came. Then we ran out beyond Gull Rock, to the nets anchored off toward the lighthouse. An hour's chumming brought no reward in the way of a strike. Whereupon we made our way back to our former location and tried there for another hour. Disappointment replaced our hopes.

R. C. and Captain Mitchell had taken their boat into Green Harbor, on the other side of Blue Island. They reported that one fisherman over there had seen a couple of tuna.

The herring were no longer abundant and had changed their locations. Some of the native fishermen were of the opinion that the fish were leaving and might not return. Others said the herring followed the bait off-shore when the wind blew from the north, and that the tuna went with them. We quit for the day.

Later we drove over to Lockeport to make inquiries there. The run of herring had slackened. The best ground at this time was between Blue Island and Western Head, and this was the place about which R. C. had been told. I was informed that a week ago one fisherman had reported a huge tuna round his net every morning. It was very tame and would just about eat out of his hand. In size it was twice as large as any seen thereabouts for some time. This was happening some six or eight miles from us, and we did not know. What an opportunity! But it seemed ungracious of me to want so much. One of an angler's weaknesses is to yearn to be in two places at the same time. I have never yet discovered any way to accomplish this. On thinking it over, however, I put this down as a natural eagerness to see more of these great tuna, and not as a dissatisfaction. The game is very hard. I would not want it otherwise.

It would not be a real test of an angler to catch some of these wonderful fish without great expense, labor, discomfort, and agony.

Sunset was a flare of red and gold, herald of a fair to-morrow. During twilight I watched several night-hawks wheeling to and fro over a swale back of the wharf. The tide was low and this hollow had only a little water. Flies or gnats of some kind must have been hovering over this particular spot. The birds flitted like streaks across the shadowy space, out over the bare bank, and all around. They came within a few feet of me, so near that I could see the white spots on their drab wings. Wonderful, graceful, eerie creatures! They did not make the slightest noise as they cut the air. They darted, whirled, flitted, infinitely faster than swallows. The irregular flight was owing to their pursuit of the gnats. They would swoop low along the ground, like an arrow, then suddenly dart upward, poise an instant, and shoot on again. As a boy I had been mystified by these strange birds. In Ohio we called them bull-bats, and they greatly resembled whippoorwills.

It struck me that I had almost forgotten my propensity to wait and watch for wild creatures. But these huge giant mackerel fish had obsessed my mind. I had forgotten that we had seen three deer on our way here. They were almost yellow, viewed against the bright wet green background, and the largest deer I had ever seen. Indeed I thought, when I sighted the first one, that it was a cow moose. But when it moved, leaping across the bank, I at once recognized that it was a buck deer. The Arizona deer are a blue-gray at this season; and these red-gold species were strikingly new and beautiful to us.

Before I turned in for the night I sat awhile in the dark over by the bridge over the cut where the tide ran in and out. It was a lonely place and a quiet hour. I heard katydids up in the woods. Lonesome and weird, they reminded me of October—of the melancholy autumn nights at Lackawaxen. Then, as if this was not enough, a frog began to boom his croaky song. He seemed to be aware of the cold and that he could not much longer bemoan the death of summer.

At three-forty-five I awoke the boys. It was cold. The moon shone with a pale brightness over the bay. There was no wind. The sea swelled in calm and peaceful movement, without any wash. The morning star burned white and large in the east, and Orion showed pale by comparison.

We had our meager breakfast, and before five o'clock were on our way down the bay. Daylight came soon. The sky was softly gray, with an open space low down in the east where the blue was kindling. Presently the gray tinged to pink and then to red. All around us the broad bay gleamed mistily, like a moving jeweled medium, and the clouds in the west took on golden crowns.

At five-thirty the sun burst up over the black forest ridge, too dazzling for my gaze. It blanched the water and caused the moon to dim. I climbed up on the bow and held to the towrope. We had reached a point between Gull Rock and Blue Island where the great swells came heaving in. How wonderful to rise on them, high and higher! We would shoot down the far slope, gliding like an arrow. Those moments were full of reward. The break of day was fair, promising. Sea and land welcomed the sun. What joy there seemed in the hour, alone there on this isolated bay, seeing and feeling the everyday life of the native fisherman!

Only two boats were sighted here between the islands,

and they reported few herring in the nets and no sign
of tuna. We ran on round Gull Rock, out into the open
sea. Here the swells lifted us seemingly on hills of sun-
glazed water. The surf pounded on the gray rocks.
Gulls screamed and wheeled around and over us, and
the snowy white-breasted gray-backed terns welcomed
us as if they remembered how we had dispensed manna
on the waters.

I saw seven boats between Gull Rock and Shelberne
Lighthouse, but they were really beyond the mouth of the
bay. We approached them. Herring showed plenti-
fully in their nets. "They've come back," said one fisherman. Another informed us no tuna had yet been
sighted. We bought our usual quantity of bait, and
asked the men to wave to us if anyone saw a tuna. In
one boat there were two men and a boy, a bright-faced
lad, very curious about us. I asked him how the herring
were running.

"Pretty good. We've got several bushel out of three
nets. And we have eight more nets to pick."

"Have you seen any tuna?" I asked.

"Not yet. But yesterday there were six around our
boat all the time we hauled. I hit one with an oar. He
was a big fellow. I'd like to see you hook him."

I knew by the way he smiled at me that he could anticipate nothing but disaster for me.

"Well, if you see one this morning you wave your
cap," I told him. "Perhaps you will have some fun
watching me."

We proceeded then toward the end of the net zone,
where our other boat had halted. Suddenly I saw R. C.
and Captain Mitchell waving to us.

"Hook her up, Cap!" I shouted.

"Shore there's somethin' doin'," remarked Bob.

It did not take many moments for us to reach the boat.

R. C. yelled and pointed. I turned to see two net-boats near at hand, and a fisherman in one of them waved to us, at the same time throwing herring overboard. Instantly a boiling swirl appeared on the water just where the herring had alighted.

"Say, did you see that?" queried Bob, turning his sharp blue glance at me.

We sped over to this boat, and Bob lifted the net-buoy out of the water and up on our bow.

"Big albacore here," said the fisherman. "He's taken two herring. I saw his head and his eye."

"Thanks for waving to us," I replied. He was a tall lean chap, dark and weather-beaten, and as he stood there in his old boat, holding the net in his hands, with fish scales shining all over his rubber clothes, I paid him a silent tribute. There is something great about fishermen who live by the sea. His boat was a low-lying launch, black with age, wet as if it had been under water. The engine box was situated in the middle. I saw scattered herring on the floor, an old oar, and a net-scoop, and several round baskets, low and flat, and ready to fall apart. All this I took in with one swift glance.

Then I threw my bait overboard, and let it drift away and sink until I could not see the end of the leader. Sid had stopped the engines. Bob was already grinding chum. I coiled fifteen feet of line on the stern, and held it in my hand, while I straddled my rod, and gazed into the beautiful green depths with fascinated eyes. I was looking to see the tuna show again. Something would happen soon, but I hardly thought I would have a bite. We all expected to see the fish come up to take one of the herring the fisherman threw out.

R. C. and Captain Mitchell and Romer stood on the deck of the other boat just outside the zone of nets, and they were observing us. The morning, the place, the situation seemed perfect for some extraordinary adventure. I felt it. Three of the fishermen's boats were near us, one just a few yards away. The men had stopped work to watch us, very curious, jovial, and with good-natured unconcealed doubt. They thought I was in for an albacore bite—and broken tackle.

Suddenly I felt a strong slow tug. The line slipped through my hand.

"He's got it!" I called. I flashed a quick glance at R. C. He waved. His sharp eyes had seen the line pay out. All the coiled line slipped overboard. I sat down, and stripped off several yards more. It was a slow sweeping movement of line. When it straightened out I jerked with all my weight and strength. The response was a tremendous downward pull on my rod. My arms cracked. My body, braced as it was by my feet against the boat, lurched over hard. Sid had the engines roaring and the launch moving. The fishermen cheered us. My line slipped off the big reel. But it did not fly off, as in the former runs. This tuna showed no lightning-swift movements at the onset. What was worse, however, he ran straight inshore toward a net. He took about two hundred feet of line before we got going satisfactorily after him. We were not saying anything. If I had spoken I could have voiced only fears. The excitement of the strike had not left me. Besides that, I had a horrible expectancy of some sure and quick calamity.

The tuna sheered just short of the net. Probably he ran to it and turned. Then he headed toward another. In fact we were hemmed in on three sides by nets. They were all within two hundred yards.

"He'll go out to sea. Don't worry," yelled Bob.

As my tuna had headed straight for another net I could not accept Bob's optimistic assertion. The action of the fish was not slow, yet it did not compare with that of the first runs of the others. We even gained a little line. When I was about to give way to despair the tuna sheered abruptly to the right. This brought our launch toward another net—the third. We had headed back almost toward the boats and the spot where I had hooked him. Hope revived in me. He might be looking for a place to get out to sea.

As good fortune would have it this tuna made another swerve away from a net, and found the lane that led out to open water. I had to whoop.

"What'd I tell you?" shouted Bob. "He didn't want to run in them nets any more than we wanted him to."

Sid bent a beaming red face upon me. "What's your legs wabbling for?" he queried. Indeed my legs were shaking, especially the right one. My knees seemed to have no bones or muscles in them. No feeling! I had not observed this proof of unusual agitation until Sid called my attention to it. But it was an old affection, not experienced for long, and it returned with a vigor and familiarity calculated to make up for absence.

The tuna got up speed; still he did not compel us to race after him. He took a couple of hundred yards of line before we regulated our pace to his. And instead of heading out to sea he took a straight course across the mouth of East Jordon Bay. It was three or four miles wide. The nets to our left were close to Gull Rock, and we soon passed them. All seemed clear sailing now. My feelings underwent change and I felt as strong as a horse. I worked so hard that the boys expressed some little fear that I might break him off.

"No danger!" I declared. "It's the lightning-swift runs that scare me. This fellow acts different. He swims deep and doesn't change his pace. But, oh! he's heavy!"

"Reckon he's a buster," observed Bob. "Suppose you try to lead him out to sea."

Whereupon we got the tuna on our port side, and while Sid edged the launch quarteringly out to sea I hauled strenuously on the rod. I lost line. Then we changed our course until I had recovered it, and tried over again. For all I could tell I did not budge him an inch from the bee line he had taken toward Blue Island. When we had covered three miles or more, and were slowly approaching the ragged black reefs reaching out from this island, I began to grow alarmed. Captain Mitchell and R. C., following us within hailing distance, waved and yelled for us to turn the fish out to sea.

"Turn this fish!" I yelled. "Ha! Ha!"

When we arrived within a half mile of the point of Blue Island we abandoned any hope of heading the tuna out to sea. He was well inside the reef now, and he might be turned up the bay.

"Boys, we'll take a chance," I decided. "If he means to go for the rocks we'll have it out with him."

Bob shook his head dubiously. He was plainly worried. Sid showed more signs of perturbation. This magnificent tuna fishing had some features not calculated to be good for one's heart.

"Run up on him," I ordered.

We closed in on the fish, and I hauled and reeled in line until we were perhaps less than two hundred feet from him. Then I shut down on the drag and set determinedly to the task ahead. The setting of this angling adventure was something on a tremendous scale, consistent with the nature of this giant tuna fighting. The south side of Blue Island showed its naked black teeth wreathed in white. Already we were lifted on the ground swells that heaved us slowly and gracefully. We were riding hills of green water. Even the fear that had begun to grip me could not wholly kill my mounting exhilaration.

Bob stood in the bow, like a mariner searching ahead for reefs. He made a strong figure standing there, his sharp-cut profile express'ng courage and intelligence.

"Shore we'll stay with him," he said. "I'm not worryin' aboot hittin' a reef. It's the line that bothers me. If it touches a rock—snap!"

"I'll go so far and no farther," replied Sid, stubbornly.

"But, man, you've got two engines heah, an' a boat followin'!" expostulated Bob. Then they argued while I toiled on that irresistible tuna. I had begun to sweat, perhaps from fright as much as exertion. For it was cold sweat! But the time and place lent me more strength than I had ever possessed before. I bent the big Murphy hickory double. I put arms, shoulders, back, and weight, with all the bracing power in my legs, into united effort to work slowly up to my limit. No sudden violence would have changed that fish. It would only have broken the tackle. My plan was to keep at him slowly and hard, all the time.

When we were a quarter of a mile off the end of the island, with my tuna heading straight in, the situation narrowed down to the climax. I had no thought then of the dramatic side of it. But I was filled with emotions freed by this struggle and the hazard, and the physical things impossible not to see and hear and feel.

Blue Island seemed a mountain, green on top, black at the sea line, a bleak jagged precipitous shore against which the great swells burst ponderously. The white spray shot high. I saw the green swells rise out of the calm sea and move in with majestic regularity, to crash and boom into white seething ruin. Then the water falling and running back off the rocks sounded like the rapids of a river. The feel of the sea under me was something at that moment to take heed of. If I had not been hooked to what must be a gigantic tuna, I would have grown panic-stricken.

"So far and no farther!" called out Sid.

"You'll do as I tell you," I replied, sharply.

"All right. If we smash it won't be my fault. I can swim," he said.

"Swim! It'd sure do you a lot of good heah," retorted Bob. "But I'm tellin' you we're safe. The big boat is just behind. Captain Mitchell is out in the skiff. Let's stay with this son-of-a-gun. He must be some fish!"

"Boys, I feel him slowing up," I called out, eagerly. "He's bumped into the bottom."

"Work all the harder then," advised Bob.

I gazed behind me to see Captain Mitchell perhaps a hundred feet from us, and beyond him the big launch rode the swells. R. C. stood in the bow. Romer waved from the deck. I could hear his shrill wild cry above the roar of the surf. Whatever else the moment held, it surely was full of stinging excitement.

We reached a point perhaps a hundred yards from the shore. It seemed closer because of the thunder of water and the looming rocks. The reef on the point stood out to our right, beyond us. Far to our left another reef extended out. Low, sharp, ugly rocks showed at times, cutting the white water.

"It's now or never," I yelled to the boys. "This is no fun. But we're in it. Now let's do the right thing, and still hang. . . . Sid, edge her off a little. We'll head him out of here or break him off."

Still I did not mean to break the tuna off. I could trust that line so long as it did not touch a rock. Putting on the small drag, something I had never done before, and screwing the larger one tighter, I increased my exertions. I determined to turn that tuna. Somehow I had not shared the opinion of the boys that the fish had gone inshore to cut off on the rocks. I pulled until at the end of every sweep I saw red. Gradually the line slipped off the reel. Gradually the launch worked her bow out from the shore. Gradually the tuna responded to the great strain put upon him. Of course the elastic rod and the perfect reel saved the line from parting. It slipped off the drags just short of the breaking point. All I had ever learned in swordfishing, about the limit of tackle strength and the conserving of muscular force, came into play here. Had I not had such long experience the task here would have been hopeless. It was a terrific fight. We dared not go any closer to where the swells smashed in green-white mounds on the rocks. I did not seem to be conscious of weakness, but I was of strain. Never had I subjected my body to such concerted and sustained effort. When I heard Bob yelling I knew we were turning the fish, though I could not hear what he said. The roar was almost deafening. Our launch glided and rose, glided on and fell, with easy motion. The violence of the seas was all inshore. Across my taut line, that sang like a telephone wire in cold wind, I saw the notched noses of the black rocks, the white seething rise and fall of foamy waves, the angry curl and break, the short spurts of water. Beyond the reef tumbled the breakers along the inside of the island. Never had a given point in my angling experiences seemed so unattainable. Only a few hundred yards! How slowly we moved! Could I last it out? I had begun that climax of this part of the fight within two hundred feet of my fish. As I worked I had lost line until over seven hundred feet were off the reel. The more feet out the more pressure on the line! It looked like a wet fiddle string and it twanged off my thumb and flipped a fine spray into my face. But hopeful indications were not wanting. The launch was not outside the danger zone, beyond the end of the reef, even if we ran straight. But the tuna had been turned broadside to the shore. That sustained me. What I had gained I would not surrender. I held to that slow, ponderous, terrific regularity of heave and wind. My sight grew dim. My heart seemed about to crack. My breast labored. My back had no sensation. I could no longer feel the bind of the leather harness.

There seems no limit to human endurance. Always I could hang on a moment longer. And I held on until my tuna rounded the end of the reef. Bob whooped the glorious news. Then I released the drags and lowered my rod to rest on the barrel of bait in front of me. Bob had stacked cushions on it. What unutterable relief! I seemed numb all over. I heard the line running off the reel, and also the accelerated working of the engines.

"Careful—slow—till I—get my breath," I panted.

"Shore. Let him have line. He's runnin' to his funeral now," shouted Bob.

The din of the surf subsided. Where dark rocks and white waves had obstructed my vision I now saw with clearing sight the wide shining waters of the bay and the beautiful forested shore line. My tuna took four hundred yards of line, with our launch going fairly fast, while I was recovering myself. Then I approached further work gradually. In half an hour I had all the line we wanted back on the reel, and we were four miles farther up the bay.

Here the large boat, with R. C. and Romer and Captain Mitchell gayly industrious with cameras of all kinds, cruised round us and up alongside.

"Must be a whopper!" yelled Romer. "Don't work too hard, dad. Don't let him get away. Don't give him any rest."

Impossible as it was to follow so much varied advice,

it struck me as being sound. I recovered surprisingly, considering the effort I had made, and soon got down to hard work again. This tuna had somehow inspired me with a conviction that he was bigger than the others. I must not spare anything. How strange it was to feel him at the end of my line, to know he was monstrous, almost unconquerable, to realize that he was indeed a tuna, though I had not had one glimpse of him. He swam deep. He never made a wave on the surface. While I fought him to the best of my reduced strength he towed the launch. Oftener and oftener Sid threw out the clutches. Then he shut off one engine entirely.

"Shore that'll take the sap out of him," declared Bob.

We seemed to be a ruthless combination of skill, cunning, experience, and strength, equipped with special instruments, all for the destruction of that poor luckless tuna. The incongruity, the unfairness of it struck me keenly. Why did I do this sort of thing? I could not answer then any more than at other times when the vexatious problem had presented itself—always at the extreme moments of the struggle. Afterward, when I asked myself the same queries, I could answer them to my satisfaction. But just then the sport seemed inhuman and unjustifiable. The psychological changes an angler goes through while fighting a fish adversary vastly his superior, the capture of which seems a vital thrilling need, are varied and extreme, some swift as flashes of emotion, and others long drawn out and compelling.

"That's a big fish," observed Bob for the twentieth time. He said it meditatively and seriously, as if talking only to himself. Bob was always thinking fish.

My tuna had developed into a more important possibility than that of the first one. I was intensely curious to have a look at him and bewailed his deep-fighting temper. He crossed the bay with us, rather close to the

Two Sisters, the only reefs in the upper waters of this harbor, and if he had turned in their direction we would have had more serious work cut out for us. But he passed by them and turned again toward the sea. This was eminently satisfactory. He took us back down the bay straight for Gull Rock. Three more miles of stubborn flight! When we got within a mile of the nets off the rock we all agreed that it was high time for us to contest this flight back toward the open sea. The brunt of such contest fell upon me. So we fought it out right there in that wide space of deep water, and I was the vanquished one. In the end I had to give in to him and let him tow us, while I confined my efforts to turning him from a straight course.

The bay here was as smooth as a mill pond, waved only by gentle swells. My tuna came up. What a wave he pushed ahead of him! Then he roared on the surface, showing first his sickle dorsal fin, then his black wide tail, then the blue bulge of his back, round as a huge tree trunk, and at last his magnificent head, out of the water to his eyes.

"Oh! Oh!" bawled Sid, wildly.

"Some socker!" ejaculated Bob. "I said he was a big fish."

To me he seemed enormous, supremely beautiful and unattainable. He flashed purple, bronze, silver-gold. When he went under he left a surging abyss in the water, a gurgling whirlpool. This sight again revived me. I was a new man, at least for a little while. I turned that tuna round. I pulled the launch toward him. I held him so that he towed us stern first. In short I performed, for the time being, miraculous and hitherto unknown feats of rod endurance. I would cheerfully have walked overboard into the sea for that fish. All the same, he took us gradually toward the nets.

The Author's World's Record Tuna, 758 Pounds (Plates xix to xxvi)

PLATE XIX

PLATE XX

PLATE XXI

PLATE XXII

PLATE XXIII

PLATE XXIV

PLATE XXV

PLATE XXVI

"They don't worry me none," said Bob, seeing my growing anxiety and dismay. "We'll go under or cut through. I was afraid of nets at first. But one end of them is free. It drifts with the tides. We can go through a dozen nets. Just you hand it to that tuna and never worry aboot nets."

Nevertheless I did worry, and I worked to the extent of all left in me. If I had not been able to slow him up, turn him from side to side, I could not have found the heart to keep it up. Many times he swerved to the surface, raising a wave that thrilled me every time I saw it. It was not a wave, but a swell. Next to that the boils that rose to the surface never ceased to fascinate me. These were new in my experience. They came when he was swimming along deep, and they would rise to the surface as far as a hundred feet behind him. They were swirls, eddies, powerful circles beginning with a small radius, and spreading until they were whirlpools six feet in diameter. More than any other single detail these breaks on the surface impressed me with the extraordinary tail power of these tuna.

I got the double line over the reel—lost it—won it back again—watched it slip away once more—heaved and wound it in—again, again, again, until my thumbs stung through gloves and stalls and my wrists and arms were pierced by excruciating pains. Still I heaved on. The ring in the wire leader came out of the water and spun round. How the leader vibrated! Bob leaped on the bow and reached for it. One last supreme effort! It took all I had left. Bent and tense, with bursting heart and failing sight, I got that leader to Bob's eager hand. When the strain was released I fell back, spent and shaking, hot and wet, absolutely all in, and most assuredly conscious of the worst beating ever given to me by a fish. I was thoroughly whipped, and so exhausted that my nerve wavered.

But seeing Bob hang to the leader reinspirited me, and so roused my thrilling wonder and speculation that I forgot my pangs. Bob would not let go. The great fish rolled and soused on the surface, thumping the water heavily. He too was tired. He could just wag his tail. But the effect of that wag pulled the launch round and round. Sid was helping to make it spin by running the engines full reverse and working the wheel. The tuna had his head toward us, and he was almost within reach of a gaff. We had to back and go round with him to keep him from going under us. Bob would haul in six or eight feet of the leader, then lose it a little at a time. I stood up the better to see. The tuna rolled on his side. And then I had my most electrifying shock. He looked as wide as a door and as long as the boat. His color was a changing blaze of silver, gold, amber, purple, and green. He seemed at once frightful and lovely, fierce and pitiful, a wild creature in the last act of precious life.

Then he changed these tactics. Righting himself, he sheered ahead and with fin out of the water he began to tow the launch. I could not see plainly. But it was evident that he could not swim otherwise than in a circle. The launch was dragged round at a fairly rapid rate, as if it were at the mercy of a strong eddy. Finally the tuna pulled the leader through Bob's hands, so that he was holding by the double line.

"Let go, Bob!" I shouted. "I'll work the leader back."

"But we'll shore have that all to do over again," objected Bob.

"No matter. Let go. I know it's tough, when you had him so near."

Bob did as he was bidden, and again the issue lay between the tuna and me. If I was weaker, so was he. I held him on the double line, so that only a few inches slipped off the reel. And he towed the launch around precisely the same as when Bob had held the leader. He came up about forty feet away, a little to the right of our bow, and turned on his side. Pale green, wonderful shieldlike shape! He was fast weakening, and that recalled my vanished strength. I thumbed the reel-drag tight as I dared, and with left gloved hand I held to the line. It cut through glove and burned my palm. But I held him. Strangely, we were all quiet now. We had seen him close. I could not look up to see where our other boat was, but I heard the beat of its engine and the cries of my faithful comrades. I could see only the shining oval fish-shape, sailing, gliding like a specter under the smooth surface. The bow of the boat and Bob's crouched form showed in the tail of my eye.

"That fish's a lost fawn-skin," yelled Bob. His quaint mode of speech and Southern twang had never struck me more forcibly. And I shared his conviction about the tuna. I felt that he was beaten. Letting go of the line, I set to heaving on the rod and whirling the reel. I could hold him, move him, drag him.

"Grab the leader, Bob," I shouted. "Sid, get ready to jump for the gaff."

A few powerful pulls brought the leader to Bob. He held it. The magnificent fish creature rolled and gaped on the surface. Bob drew on the leader, inch by inch at first, then, when he got the tuna coming, foot by foot, until he was close to the bow, head toward us, swimming on his side while Sid backed the boat. When I gave the word Sid threw out the clutch, leaped over the engine box, and grasping the gaff he leaned far over—and lunged back. The detachable gaff pole came loose, leaving the rope in Sid's hands, but the pole hit him hard over the head. He yelled lustily, as mad as if one of us had done it with intent. I could not see the tuna now, but I heard him begin to splash and pound, harder, faster, until the water flew above us and I could scarcely see Bob.

"Did he make a good job of it?" I yelled, fearfully.

"Shore. We got him. An' I'll have a rope round his tail in a jiffy," replied Bob.

That gave me license to sit down and let go of the rod, so suddenly a burden. The other boat came up and we were hailed and cheered. Captain Pence waved the British flag. Presently Bob had the tuna safely lassoed and tied to our stern, where the ponderous thumps from a mighty tail splashed water over me.

"Three hours an' ten minutes!" exclaimed Bob, consulting his watch.

"Seemed a year to me," I replied, but I did not tell them then how that tuna had punished me.

"Well, let's go home," spoke up Sid, brightly. "The little launch and the big tackle sure are the dope."

"Wal, where do we all come in?" drawled Bob.

It took us nearly two hours to tow our catch back up the bay to the breakwater. Every time I looked at him I was sure he grew larger in my sight. When we reached the wharf our eager comrades almost fell overboard to see that fish.

We rigged up three poles with block and tackle, and prepared to haul the tuna up on the wharf. I told Captain Mitchell that I had beaten his world record of 710 pounds. I had no way of knowing, yet somehow I felt absolutely sure of it.

"I hope you have," replied Mitchell, studying the blue-and-silver monster lying in the water.

The men had a hard time hauling the fish up, and as he came more and more into sight his enormous size grew manifest. Moreover, for me there was something appallingly beautiful about him. At last they had him high enough to lower on the wharf. Then I was mute! I could not believe my own sight.

"What a grand tuna!" ejaculated Captain Mitchell, in heartfelt admiration and wonder. "Indeed you have beaten my record. . . . Old man, I congratulate you. I am honestly glad."

They all had something fine to say to me, but I could not reply. I seemed struck dumb by the bulk and beauty of that tuna. My eyes were glued to his noble proportions and his transforming colors. He was dying, and the hues of a tuna change most and are most beautiful at that time. He was shield-shaped, very full and round, and high and long. His back glowed a deep dark purple; his side gleamed like mother-of-pearl in a lustrous light; his belly shone a silver white. The little yellow rudders on his tail moved from side to side, pathetic and reproachful reminders to me of the life and spirit that was passing. If it were possible for a man to fall in love with a fish, that was what happened to me. I hung over him, spellbound and incredulous.

"Well, I always said it was coming to you," averred R. C., and I gauged his appreciation by his tone and the significance of his words.

The native fishermen who lived near the breakwater came down to see the tuna. I was most eager to get their point of view. Frank Sears had been there for fifteen years and had been recommended to me as a man of integrity and intelligence. One of his men had fished for herring along that coast all his life. These fishermen had seen thousands of albacore, as they called the tuna. They walked round him, from one side to the other, and the more they gazed the keener were my thrills and anticipations.

"Biggest albacore I ever saw," said Sears, at length. "He's got a small head. He's all body, and big and thick clear down to his tail. We have shipped over two hundred albacore to the markets and have had hundreds in the traps and weirs. But that's the biggest I ever saw. You might fish for ten years and never see another like it."

Sears's man was even more gratifying. "I can say the same. He'll go over eight hundred pounds. Fish are my business and I'm not given to overestimating. . . . You certainly must have caught the big one that's been seen around Western Head for a month or more."

When I exhibited my tackle to these fishermen their interest and amaze knew no bounds. They could hardly believe so huge and powerful a fish, the kind that had often smashed their boats, gone through net and weir, could have been held and subdued on that little line. In truth the thirty-nine-thread line did look small, but its strength was mighty.

My tuna was 8 feet 8 inches in length, 6 feet 4 inches in girth. His head measured 2 feet and 5 inches in length. Yet Sears had called his head small. He weighed 758 pounds.

Perhaps my son's remark pleased me most of all:

"Sure is some fish! Biggest ever caught on a rod, by anybody, any kind of a game fish. . . . And I was here to see you lick him, dad!"

Mr. Sears signed an affidavit for me, substantiating his statements above, and Captain Mitchell wrote another for me as follows:

EAST JORDON, NOVA SCOTIA,
August 22, 1924.

To ANYONE IT MAY CONCERN:
This is to certify that I was one of the eight men who saw Mr. Zane Grey's 758-pound tuna fought, landed, and weighed.

It broke my record tuna weight, 710 pounds, which I have held for some years. And I confirm the statement made by Sears and the native fishermen here.

(Signed)   CAPTAIN LAURIE D. MITCHELL.

That evening there was a rather pale and threatening sunset. The bay became as calm as a mill pond. But before dark a slight ripple moved from the southeast and a damp wind followed it. Then a ring appeared round the moon. We were in for more weather.

And the next day it rained. Moreover, although it rained hard all day it did not really get started until night. Then there was a deluge. We passed a most uncomfortable night.

The following morning fog and rain obscured all but the closest objects. During the afternoon rain fell at intervals, drizzling and misty, and the fog curtain blew in, sometimes dense, at others permitting sight of the island and headlands. We put in the time as best we could, mostly playing checkers with the insatiable Romer. He succeeded in beating all of us once, to his great joy.

The next morning we fished in the fog. Herring had become very scarce, and likewise tuna. Later in the day we learned that some fishermen had taken a good number of herring off Blue Island, and one of these men reported having tuna around his boat. The fishermen between Gull Rock and Shelberne Light caught no herring at all, and were convinced the run was about over. We were inclined to agree with this opinion, but decided to try another morning off Blue Island.

During the afternoon the fog lifted somewhat and we had a few hours of less depressing weather. Upon returning from a walk I found Romer fishing, and as I approached I saw him haul a small, big-headed fish up on the wharf, very gingerly detach it from his hook, and cast it back into the water. Then he flipped his bait back.

[97]

As his action was unusually interesting I went over to his side with a query as to his luck.

"Sculpin! Darndest fish I ever saw!" he ejaculated, disgustedly.

"How so?" I inquired.

"I've caught that sculpin five times. He's a big hog and a darn fool, I'll say."

"Romer, surely you are mistaken! You haven't caught the same fish five times?"

"You just bet I have," he declared. "See here! Look! . . . There! I've got him again."

Whereupon he jerked out a queer, ugly, misshapen fish about a foot in length, gray and black, with large head and enormous mouth. Somehow the name sculpin seemed felicitous. Romer had the fish hooked squarely through the thick jaw. He handled it most carefully, explaining to me that the sculpin had poisonous spines, very dangerous, the sting of which had cost boys loss of arm and even life. His hook was large and not easily extracted.

"Now, watch," he said, throwing the sculpin back into the water and dropping hook and bait after it. I did indeed watch, and I saw the fish swim round with slow motion, apparently unconcerned about having been hooked and hauled out six times. Romer edged his bait near where the sculpin was circling, not far under the surface. When it saw the bait it promptly opened that huge mouth. I was amazed. That sculpin showed no instinct of self-preservation except the one of feeding. It took the large bait ravenously. Romer jerked hard and hauled the crazy fish up for the seventh time.

"Say, what do you know about that?" he inquired.

"Well, to tell the truth, Romer, I don't know anything," I replied. "That is a stumper. I wonder what naturalists would say. No doubt the sight of food acts so powerfully upon the senses of a sculpin that no other reaction is possible. . . . Throw him back again."

The identical performance was repeated for my benefit, and to my further mystification and wonder. There are many low forms of life in the sea, and a sculpin, although he is a fish, must indeed belong to one of them. Stupidity would seem to be his dominant characteristic, and hoggishness his strongest instinct. It would be interesting to learn what enemies a sculpin has, if any, and how he reacts to them.

Next morning we were up at four, in the cool damp dark grayness. The fog had raised. I could see the black fringe of the forests. But the stars were obscured. At daylight we were bound across the bay to meet a native fisherman, Harold Locke, who had left out a herring net in our interest. He was waiting for us on his little dock, beneath a tiny gray cottage on the hill. He lived, indeed, beside the sea and by the sea. I liked his clean-cut lean face, tanned by exposure, and his tall form, clad in soiled rubber overalls. He was not optimistic as to the herring. And indeed his net yielded only a few bait.

We ran round to the net-buoys on the other side of Gull Rock. The nets had been taken up. Much disappointed, we crossed the mouth of the bay, pushing into an incoming bank of fog. Only one fishing boat could we find, and the men in this informed us that the herring and albacore had gone out to sea. So we gave up and decided to return to Liverpool.

On our way up the bay we ran out of the fog into bright sunshine, a very welcome and beautiful change. But the wind appeared to be rising. After putting Locke ashore we turned back down the bay. Blue Island and Gull Rock were disappearing in a low silver fog bank. But as it looked broken and moving out to sea we ventured to go on. What a strange difference when we entered that gray, cool, mystic medium! It changed all. Here it was thick and there thin. Sometimes the sun would shine through and again we were engulfed in a heavy wet blanket. We followed the shore line, however, all the way out to Western Head, and as we rounded that low dark booming point we ran into thick mist. We should have turned back. But as we had run into and out of fog I decided we might risk it by laying a course for the whistling-buoys along the coast.

Captain Pence laid his course, but it led us straight into the reefs. And it was my sharp eye that first espied the dim black edges of rock. We slowed down, changed our course, and then ran between and around the rocks, out to sea. I shall not soon forget that strained two hours.

Again we came out of the fog bank, so that we could see the rocky shore line. All seemed well then. We ran on. But the sea began to rise with the wind, and in an hour it was rough, too rough for our small launch. We could not have fought our way against it. With a following sea, however, we bowled along, shipping only a little water.

Good luck could not stand by us. The large boat, which we had engaged solely as a safeguard for our little launch, slowly dropped astern and finally stopped. Something was wrong. Bob and Sid certainly said some things about the single-action engine in that boat. But danger or no danger, we had to put back to their aid. The way we tossed on the huge waves frightened me. We managed to reach them and take off R. C. and Romer. Captain Pence yelled that his engine would not run and he could not start it. Bob boarded the boat and soon yelled to us: "Out of gas!" That was not all he yelled.

There was nothing to do but attempt to tow the boat. I knew it would not be easy. When Sid asked me for orders I realized the danger. We got a long line to them, and then ran before the sea. The towline broke our stern gunwale and pulled out the braces, so that we had to tie to the fishing chair. I feared the strain would pull out the whole back end of the launch. But it held. We headed in for the entrance of the harbor of Port Joli, the place so famous as a winter feeding grounds for wild geese.

When we finally entered the harbor and were sighted by fishermen from shore, my relief was immense. Gas was procured, and the trip to Liverpool made without further mishap.

It rained hard that night. And next day was dismal, wet, dark. Toward evening the wind increased and the rain beat. When I went to bed it was pouring. About one o'clock I was awakened by the shaking of the house and the roaring of wind. A storm had burst upon us. I could not go back to sleep. Indeed, in an hour I did not want to. The lights went out, so that the whole place was in total darkness. I lay listening to the lash of rain, the roar of wind, the crash of breaking branches and falling trees. And presently I realized that it was a hurricane. I remembered then that I had seen the dock lined by fishing smacks which had run in that day. But surely all boats and ships had not made some safe port. I knew that somewhere out there in the roaring ebony blackness mariners and fishermen were at the mercy of the elements.

I lay awake until dawn, when the fury of the storm abated. It had lasted four hours and had been the worst in my experience. When I went out I found the streets almost impassable for wires and fallen trees. Much damage had been done. I walked down to the park, where the little lighthouse stood, and there I gazed out over the bay toward the open sea.

A pale sun was rising. The black clouds were sweeping away before a shifting wind. On the reefs great combers were breaking, green and white. The cold bright Atlantic Main! I did not on the moment feel any love for it. It cleared off and the day became fine, with a brisk northwest breeze.

Not until next day did we learn much of what a fearful storm it had been. Then tales of wrecked ships and missing men came in, all the way from Halifax to the Bay of Fundy. That jagged shallow shore, cut like the teeth of a saw, and the fiercest driving sea seen for years, had exacted a frightful toll of loss and life. I read of several wonderful rescues by shore fishermen, one particularly filling me with awe and reverence for the single fisherman who at terrible risk of his life had saved the crew of a trawler. And it is the modern trawlers that are driving the shore fishermen out of business. How heroic, such a man! But somehow it is good to know. This storm made clearer to me the lives of these fishermen. I understood then the quiet lean faces, the pondering brows, the sad eyes, the lack of something that I might call joy of life. For them life was as hard as the relentless sea. It made them pay.

After this storm the weather cleared beautifully. Today, which is the third since the havoc wrought by wind and sea, the fishermen came in from their nets and traps with boatloads of mackerel and the first of the spawning herring. Tuna were reported at the mouth of the harbor.

Several other ambitious anglers have arrived from Boston and New York. They have come poorly equipped, and like all former anglers who have visited Nova Scotia, they have no idea of the difficulty of this game. I tried not to discourage them. It is always a delicate matter—trying to advise anglers. I never do

it any more unless requested, and even then I am reluc-
tant. Fishermen are queer. They are fundamentally
egoists. They cannot, as a class, be instructed. Those
who excel, that is to say, who learn to fish, do so through
a long, slow, painful process. Salt-water fishing for
huge fish is not casting a salmon fly or sitting on a green
bank with a pole and line. It is strenuous, and this
Nova Scotia tuna angling is extraordinarily trying. One
angler said: "Oh, I'll be satisfied to break a few off!"
Another expressed the amazing opinion that it would be
well to have a long lever attached to a reel, so that by
a forward and back movement the line could be drawn in.
And then one of the Liverpool boatmen told how the
angler he had taken out several years ago, and who had
lost so many tuna, had hooked his fish, or had claimed
to hook them. He used a cork on his line some four feet
above the leader. An ordinary small net cork, about five
inches in diameter! According to this angler, when a
tuna took his bait and pulled the cork under, the cork
hooked the fish. This was an actual statement. It
rendered me speechless. You could not drive a nail
into the jaw of a tuna without a hammer and considerable force. My brother, using my heavy tackle, and
striking with all his great shoulder strength, had failed
three times to set the hook in the jaws of these tuna.

I may have some remarkably interesting things to
record here before many days pass.

Next morning we were up at four-thirty, and on the
way down the bay before sunrise. The morning was
clear, crisp, cool, with rosy east and sky a pale blue.

We found fishermen pulling their nets and traps, but
herring were scarce. At length we obtained half a
bushel or more, and went to chumming near a trap where
the men were taking off a good catch of mackerel. The

swells rolled in from the open sea, not by any means comfortable. In fact this place was almost out in the open.

We saw a tuna smashing the water near the trap next
to the one where we were anchored, and we made haste
to run over there. Two of the anglers mentioned above
were near by in boats, and evidently sighted the tuna
also, for they made for the trap as quickly as possible.
Whereupon we were soon all fishing for that tuna.

"Reckon there'll be a tackle funeral round heah if
business picks up," observed Bob.

Soon we left to run over behind Coffin Island, a very
felicitously named rock-bound bit of treacherous land,
catching fairly the brunt of the sea roll. We tried here
awhile, and then ran to a point off Port Medway, where
Captain Mitchell had done most of his fishing. He
showed us the place where he had hooked his 710-pound
tuna. We anchored outside another trap, a large one,
and began to chum as usual. The sun shone bright; the
gulls screamed and laughed; the terns flitted about for
bits of our ground-up herring. The sea was heaving and
as clear as crystal. What a spectacle it would have been
to see a tuna rise for a bait in this clear water! But it
was not to be.

This trap interested me. It was made of seine twine,
with corks and buoys keeping it afloat. The body lines
somewhat resembled a huge figure 8, two hundred feet
or more in length. The wings extended a long way ob-
liquely from the trap. When herring or mackerel encountered these wings they swam along them, and so
entered the small hole into the maze of net partitions,
and seldom or never found their way out again. The
same could be said of the tuna that entered. These trap
fishermen, however, preferred to open the nets and let
out the huge fish. It was cheaper to allow them to

escape. It took six men in three boats to tend the trap. They reported a few mackerel and no herring or tuna.

On the way back to Liverpool Bay we passed a storm-battered fishing smack, returning from the banks. She certainly showed scars of struggle with the hurricane. We learned, later, that one man had been lost overboard. Two schooners came into Lunenburg that day, with flags at half mast, and both captains reported loss of life and much damage in the worst storm of their sea experience. A number of fishing schooners had not yet been heard from. Assuredly some of them had been lost. It struck me to the heart, the tragedy of these fishermen's lives. Yet they are not hardened. They are serious seafaring folk, religious and simple in their lives, as indeed are most men who live in the open and fight the elements. I could not help but try to picture in mind the fury of the storm, the black night, and the terrible white horses of the sea, crashing over the vessels and carrying away boats, spars, and men. These heroic fishermen faced death every time they left home. And some of them had met it. Man overboard! Perhaps he was not even missed in the grim wild moment. But he knew! When he was swept away into the black night, on the crest of a crashing wave, he knew his doom. How tremendous and sickening to think of, and yet how splendid! He was washed overboard. He would swim and fight for his life, as a brave man, when all the time he would know. Surely he would pray. There would be thought of home, wife, children. . . . And then—!

On Sunday morning I arose early and went out for a walk. It was a quiet, peaceful, beautiful morning. The streets were deserted. Not a sign of life! I walked to the park at the end of the street, and sat near the lighthouse, facing down the bay.

At once I was struck with the remarkable tranquillity and repose of the scene. Never had I seen such an unruffled surface of water. It was like silk. Only at the shoals near the beach did any motion show, and that was a gentle, almost indistinguishable swell. The bay shone a dark pearl-gray color, mirroring the clouds. Had it not been for the dark-green rugged shores stretching away to the east, and the lighthouse marking the headland, there would not have been any telling sea and sky apart. Not a breath of wind! How strange that seemed after the recent hurricane! It was only another mood of the inscrutable ocean. Almost I loved it then. But I could not forget. I think the ocean fascinates me, draws me, compels me, but not with love. By listening intently I caught a faint low roar of surf far outside the headlands, and then the moaning of the whistle buoy, and at last the melancholy ring of a bell buoy. The spell of the scene gripped me and was difficult to explain. There was no sign of sunrise, though the hour was long past. A pale purple bank of cloud rose above the dim horizon line. Toward the south it broke and lightened, until a clearer space shone with some hue akin to rose and pearl. The whole effect seemed one of lull before a storm, and I was reminded that another hurricane had struck off the Virgin Islands and was reported traveling north. While I sat there, watching, listening, feeling, a strong desire to return to Nova Scotia at some future time moved me to vow that I would. It was indeed a far cry from California. Nevertheless I found myself planning another trip to this land of spruce forests and rock-lined streams of amber water, to this wild storm-bound coast with its beautiful bays and coves, its thundering reefs and lonely gale-swept headlands.

III

A RECORD FIGHT WITH A SWORDFISH

ON the very first day of our 1919 season, July 1st, my brother R. C. and I, with Captain Danielson, had the longest and hardest swordfish battle on record.

Come to think of it, there are on record really very few battles with broadbill swordfish. To be sure, many of the old gladiators of the sea have been hooked by random Catalina anglers, but swordfishermen themselves do not credit the many instances where some one happened to hook a broadbill and fought it for a few moments or per- haps longer. As a matter of fact, few novices at the game ever held a broadbill longer than a few moments. Credit has gone to the few men who deliberately go out after broadbills, and keep on going day after day for weeks and months.

Old *Xiphias gladius* is the noblest warrior of all the sea fishes. He is familiar to all sailors. He roams the Seven Seas. He was written about by Aristotle 2,300 years ago. In the annals of sea disasters there are records of his sinking ships. In the logs of many mariners have been found accounts of this old swordfish attacking ships and sending them back to port for repairs. Tales of his attacks on harpooners' boats in the Atlantic are common. In these waters, where he is hunted for the market, he has often killed his pursuers. In the Pacific, off the Channel Islands, he has not killed any angler or boatman yet, but it is a safe wager that he will do so some day. Therefore, despite the wonderful nature of the sport, it is not remarkable that so few anglers have risked it. Of all the Tuna Club anglers there are only five who have won the gold-and-white broadbill swordfish button—Boschen, Adams, Johnson, Farnum, and myself.

July 1st seemed the most perfect of days. All Avalon days are perfect, but this day was something to make a man keen to the joy of life and the beauty of nature. A fisherman's hopes are of the future and his joys are of the present.

The fog broke up and rolled away early that morning, letting the sunshine down bright and warm. The sky shone azure blue, and the sea under it a deeper blue. Dark, glancing ripples, here and there with crests of white, waved regularly away before the west wind.

We took my boy Romer with us, and the occasion was his initial experience on the sea. I hoped to make a fisherman of him, but, alas, in his ten years of existence, he had not yet shown any remarkable tendencies toward that end. Romer's idea of fishing, like that of many grown-up men I know, was to sit on a rock or a bank or a dock—some sure, steady, safe place—and throw a lot of baited hooks into the water, and pull out fish until he had caught more than anybody else. Upon this occasion it was difficult to persuade Romer that he was merely a guest and somewhat fortunate to be that.

By eleven o'clock we were way up the channel, about six miles from land, directly opposite a deep cut-in in the rocky shore named Catalina Harbor. The west wind had softened to a light breeze; the sea was flattening out, dimpled and blue, with long, low swells running. Captain Dan was up on top, watching for swordfish fins on the surface; Romer was in the cabin; R. C. had a keen eye on the ocean; and I was lazily holding my rod, dozing in my chair, contentedly yielding to the warm sun, the motion of the boat, and the sweet, soft scent of the sea.

Suddenly R. C. murdered this peacefulness. "Swordfish!" he bellowed.

Captain Dan's heavy feet thumped on the cabin deck above, and he yelled; Romer came running out, with his shrill treble voice at top key; R. C. stood up, alert, erect, with stiff arm pointing seaward. "Look! Are they fins or sails of a schooner? Look! If that's not a broadbill I'll eat him!"

"Broadbill all right—and a buster!" boomed Captain Dan as he threw out the clutch. "Wind in your baits and let me put on fresh flying fish."

Whereupon I came out of my trance and beheld the dark, sickle-shaped fins of a swordfish riding the slow swells some three hundred yards out. The sight gave me an inexplicable thrill. Then a bursting gush of blood warmed my sluggish veins. I hurried to wind in my bait.

All was now cheerful excitement on board that boat. Captain Dan put a new bait, a fine fat flying fish, on R. C.'s hook, throwing it overboard and heading the boat to cross in front of the swordfish, so as to drag the bait before his eyes. When we got to within a hundred yards of the fish I began to think that he was pretty big. His fins looked large, but they were partially submerged. The distance from dorsal fin to tail began to amaze me. Still I was too pleasantly excited to be sure of anything. R. C. had made some wonderful catches of Marlin or roundbill swordfish the preceding years, but he had never even hooked a broadbill. Captain Dan and I were exceedingly anxious to try out his mettle on an old gladiator. R. C.'s remarkable catch of seven Marlin in one day had rather made us want to see him hooked to the bottom of the ocean or to some big fish that he could not haul in right away.

I climbed up on top of the deck so that I could see better. As the boat passed the swordfish, perhaps two hundred feet distant, I could plainly see the dark, purple, rounded mass of his body, big as a barrel, it seemed, in the clear water. He was drifting lazily and did not know that there was a boat within a mile. At that moment there never occurred to me the chances against a strike, and the further chances against hooking him if he did strike, and still further the almost impossible chance of whipping him even if he did get hooked.

When the bait reached a point about fifty feet ahead of him, he gave his tail a flirt and moved forward, to sink in a swirl of water. I believed that he meant to take R. C.'s bait. Most assuredly at least he meant to look it over.

Suddenly the line whipped up off the water. It was the motion given to a fishing line by the swordfish when he strikes the bait with his sword. No other fish in the sea gives a line such a strange and thrilling motion!

"He's got it!" whispered R. C.

Then we all watched the line slip off the reel. At first it went slowly, then gradually faster. R. C.'s face wore a pleasant, satisfied smile of excitement.

"Hook him! Hook him!" boomed Captain Dan, with a deep ring in his heavy voice. It reminded me that he and I both had seen broadbills hooked before.

R. C. threw on the drag and lowered the rod while the line straightened; he squared his powerful shoulders and jerked back with all his might. Both rod and line seemed to crack. But they held. R. C. swept forward and heaved back.

"That's the way," boomed Captain Dan. "Soak him! . . . Fast an' hard now! . . . He's comin' up! See the line?"

The moment was one of great stress. I knew that R. C. had hooked a broadbill, yet I could not believe it. With strained eyes I watched the line rise and rise, until the spot where it led my sight burst into a white, crashing splash, in the midst of which a huge, obscure, purple body flashed. The swordfish did not show well, but he showed that he was hooked. He threshed around in foam, with only his sword in sight, banging at the wire leader. Then, with a heavy swirl, he sounded between four and five hundred feet, and stayed down there, slowly working seaward. We kept after him, but R. C. did not recover any line.

"Well, Red, he's comin' up," said Dan, cheerfully. "He doesn't like it down there. Now go to work on him."

I think these last words of Captain Dan's brought reality to me. To go to work on a broadbill meant a great deal. I knew. It meant to lift and haul and pump with the rod, to lower the tip swiftly and wind the reel desperately, and to repeat that performance over and over, endlessly, until sight and muscle almost failed. When R. C. came up hard and fast the first time with his powerful sweep, I made the startling discovery that the rod he was using was my light Marlin rod. I gasped with surprise and groaned inwardly with despair. How on earth did it happen that he had hooked the swordfish on that rod? The simple fact was that we had neglected to have him use the heavy rod.

To be sure, the little Murphy rod had long ago proved its wonderful quality, but it was not stiff enough for a broadbill. There was danger of breaking. And after a while I had to caution R. C. about this. He did not seem to let up any. Every time he heaved back with all his weight in the action, the rod described a half circle, and the line twanged like a banjo string. It was take and give. He would recover a hundred feet or so, and then the broadbill would run that much out again. He came up to thresh and roll and swish on the surface, showing only his fins and sword. He fought heavily and sluggishly. And at the end of an hour he appeared to be tiring. R. C. saved nothing of his strength then, and worked harder and harder. The big fish fought for every foot of line, but slowly he was dragged closer and closer. R. C. was hot and wet and panting now. Every time he leaned back and bent the rod double I thought he would crack it. Captain Dan's dubious face attested to the same fear. Yet both of us hated to warn him further. It was not until the swordfish was within thirty feet of the boat that either of us yielded to our dread. I was the first to see the fish. He looked a long, indistinct, purple mass. Climbing up on deck, I got a better sight of him. I could not be sure just how big he was, but I could tell that he was very large. R. C. dragged him closer inch by inch. He was swimming at right angles with the boat. His outline grew clearer. The end of the double line next the wire leader appeared on the surface of the water.

"Careful, Red!" warned Captain Dan. "That's an awful strain."

"I can—bring him—to gaff," panted R. C., grimly.

"Fellows, he's bigger than you have any idea," I called from my vantage point. "Ease up or you'll break the rod."

R. C let up on the strain and the swordfish rolled away and down out of sight. This caution of mine might have been a blunder. R. C. always insisted afterward that he could have brought the swordfish to gaff then. For my part, I am positive he would have broken the rod. But I will say that if he had been using the heavier Murphy rod he would have brought that magnificent swordfish up to the boat. Broadbills do not wake up until they have been worked on for a few hours.

"Aw, why didn't you let Uncle Rome pull him in?" complained Romer, bitterly. "Now we'll never get him back."

It did seem that he presaged the truth. Our quarry changed his tactics. He had been slow; now he became fast. He had stayed down rather deep; now he came to the surface. First he made a long run, splashing over the swells. We had to put on full power to keep up with him, and at that he took off a good deal of line. When he slowed up he began to fight the leader. He would stick his five-foot sword out of the water and bang the leader. Then he lifted his enormous head high and wagged it from side to side, so that his sword described a circle, smacking the water on his left and then on his right. Wonderful and frightful that sweep of sword! It would have cut a man in two or have pierced the planking of a boat. Evidently his efforts and failure to free himself roused him to fury. His huge tail thumped out of great white boils; when he turned sideways he made a wave like that behind a ferryboat; when he darted here and there he was as swift as a flash and he left a raised bulge, a white wake on the surface. Suddenly he electrified us by leaping. Broadbill swordfish seldom clear the water after being hooked. They leap, however, at other times. This one came out in a tremendous white splash, and when he went down with a loud crash we all saw where the foam was red with blood. Captain Dan yelled in surprise at his size. R. C. did not show any surprise and he kept silent. I took out my thrilling excitement in a mad scramble for my camera. Before I could get ready the swordfish leaped again, a magnificent leap that I would give anything to have photographed. Like a leaping tuna, he shot out slick and clean. But when he dropped back he made a thunderous smash on the water.

He leaped again, almost all the way out, and was half obscured in spray. I snapped the camera on him. Then he seemed to want to perform for my benefit. He lashed a great patch of water into white foam; he surged and went down with his wonderful broad flukes high in the air; he came up and up and up, with his black rapier straight to the sky; he fell over on his side to smack the water. Then he leaped again.

There was no use trying to hold him or fight him while he was up to such tricks. All we could do was to chase him. Half the time R. C.'s line lay slack, and often it had a wide bag in it. He did not even try to keep a tight line.

"Say! he's comin' at us!" yelled the boy. And indeed Romer was the first to become aware of possible peril.

"Wait, Dan! Don't run away from him yet," I begged.

It may have been foolhardy of me, but I could not resist the thrilling opportunity. To see that swordfish throwing water like a motor boat, headed for us, with his wicked bill in the air, was a sight to freeze the blood of any angler who could recognize the danger. In that rush of perhaps a hundred yards he leaped three times, only

THE GREAT BROADBILL (Plates xxvii to xxxii)

(This is the fish whose battle for freedom lasted eleven-and-a-half hours.)

PLATE XXVII

PLATE XXVIII

PLATE XXIX

PLATE XXX

PLATE XXXI

PLATE XXXII

one leap of which I caught with the camera. Then he sounded. But he stayed down only a few seconds. I saw the water bulge closer to us. Then further on his black sword shot up out of a smooth place, and then his green-and-silver head, showing his great black eye, and then his purple body, huge and round and glistening. With back toward us he rose about three-quarters of his length, and in a cloud of flying spray seemed to hang there a second. I made the best of this opportunity. When he soused back he swerved toward us again. If I had not been scared before, I certainly was then. "Run away from him!" I yelled to Captain Dan.

We lost no time getting away from where he was smashing the water white. Then, at about three hundred yards, we stopped, with the stern of the boat toward him, and there we watched the conclusion of his mad rushes and leaps. In all he leaped fourteen times, several leaps of which were wholly clear of the water. But these, the greatest chances I ever had to take incomparable pictures, I missed. Too slow and overanxious! At length he settled down and with a sullen swirl ended his surface pyrotechnics.

R. C. began slowly to recover line, and for two more hours heaved like a Trojan, never resting a moment, never letting the rod down on the gunwale. But he did not get the hundred-foot mark on the line over the reel again. The swordfish had been hooked at 11.30. At 3.30 R. C. had expended the best of his efforts. That was plain. He was in bad shape. Wet, hot, dirty, disheveled, he looked, indeed, as if he had been in a fight. Moreover, he began to get that greenish cast of face which portends seasickness.

"Will you take the rod?" he asked me.

I refused, but his request worried me exceedingly. I knew then that he was in worse shape than he looked.

The afternoon wind was springing up, making the boat roll. It is hard enough to fight a swordfish in a smooth sea, but when the fish is underneath and the boat is rising on the waves, then the fight becomes something indescribable. I exhausted all my eloquence (and I guess wasted it) upon R. C. Captain Dan talked and talked. R. C. saved his breath and worked wearily on the rod. His face had turned a pale green. At 4.30 he rolled and swayed at his task. "I'm all in," he said, faintly. "If I hadn't got—seasick—maybe I'd have licked him. Maybe. Take the rod!"

R. C. let the rod down on the gunwale for the first time, and while I held it firmly in the seat socket, he got up. As he went into the cabin he staggered. Captain Dan looked very gloomy.

When I straddled the rod and took the seat I was as furious at the swordfish as I was sorry for R. C. I intended to make short work of that swordfish. Romer said: "I'll bet you can't pull him right up." It struck me then how little boys have an uncanny divination at times. I braced myself with feet against the gunwale, squared my shoulders, clamped my gloved thumbs down on the line, and heaved with all my might. Then I felt the heaviest live weight that it had ever been my fortune to have at the end of a fishing line. Ponderous, irresistible, it gave me a shock. Doubt at once assailed me. This swordfish was unbeatable. But that did not keep me from exerting myself. Fresh and strong, I began to lift and wind. It gratified me to see that I could lift him little by little. It took just thirty minutes for me to lift our quarry so that we could see the hundred-foot mark on the line. Then he anchored himself at that depth and I could not budge him. Not another foot did I gain. Worse than this, if I did not lift desperately and hold desperately he slowly sank deeper, taking more line. All the time he worked out to sea.

Two hours passed by swiftly. However laborious and painful they were they did not drag. I toiled at that job. I spent myself in those two hours, and then, dripping wet, smarting and burning, out of breath, numb, and almost strengthless, I had to rest. Old *Xiphias* sank a couple of hundred feet, and apparently satisfied with that depth he tugged on out to sea.

At sunset the wind died away and the sea quieted down. It gave me a good deal of comfort, but I did not imagine it added anything to my chances of getting the fish. The sun set behind broken clouds of gold and silver and purple. Long rays of rare blue, fan shape and sharply defined, spread toward the zenith. The sea seemed divided by a radiant track of golden light. The west end of Catalina Island, with its rugged mountains, took on crowns of like color and glory. Clemente Island lay a dark, lonely strip of land, fading in the twilight.

By and by darkness stole over the ocean and all was obscure save in the west, where a pale afterglow marked the sunset. At seven-thirty I passed the rod to Captain Dan. He was as eager to take it as I was to give it, and he began to work on the swordfish. Big and powerful as he was, he could not subdue that swordfish. He pulled as hard as he dared, and at every pull I said good-by to the rod. But it did not break. Many times Captain Dan got the swordfish within the hundred feet, but that was all. At nine-thirty he was tired.

"Whale of—a broadbill!" panted Dan. "He's one that's swallowed the first one we had on. What'll we do?"

"Let's both work on him," I suggested.

So, standing beside Dan, a little in front, I grasped the rod above where he held it, and heaved with him. I had rested, and aside from having pretty sore hands I was all right again. R. C. and Romer saw us from the cabin and called for us to pull the fish in or break something. Most assuredly I expected something to break. But it did not. That was the wonder of the whole fight. We both pulled in unison as hard as we could upon that rod. It bent double, but did not break.

R. C. groaned as he watched.

"Oh! if you'd only let me pull like that when I had him near the boat!"

I groaned also, and I was angry with myself and sick of the whole business. But it was too late. I think Captain Dan and I both had a sneaking hope that we would break him off, and then we could go back to Avalon. We were wet, cold, hungry. No fun, no sport any more!

The two of us working together, began to tell on the swordfish. We stopped him. We turned him. We got him coming. Still we could not tell how close we had him. The 150-foot mark had worn off the line. Then, just when our hopes began to mount and we began to believe that we could whip him, the great reel went out of gear. The drag refused to stick. Dan could wind in the line, but there was no drag to hold it. He had to hold it with his thumbs. This was heartbreaking. Yet we seemed to rise to a frenzy and worked all the harder.

At eleven o'clock, in spite of our handicap, we had the swordfish coming again. It looked as if we had the best of him. Eleven and one-half hours! It did seem as if victory would crown our combined efforts. But we were both well-nigh exhausted and had to finish him quickly if we were to do it at all. The sea was dark now. A wan starlight did not help us, and we could not always tell just where our quarry was. Suddenly, to our amazement, he jerked the line from under Dan's thumbs and made a magnificent run. Then the line slacked. "He's off!" exclaimed Dan. I told him to wind. He did so, getting nearly all the line back. Then the old strain showed again on the rod. Our broadbill had only changed his tactics. He made some sounding thumps on the surface. "Say, I don't like this," said Dan. "He's runnin' wild."

I was reminded that Boschen, Adams, and myself all agreed on the theory that broadbill swordfish wake up and become fierce and dangerous after dark. This one certainly verified that theory. In the dark we could not tell where he was, whether he was close or near, whether he menaced us or not. Some of the splashes he made sounded angry and close. I expected to hear a crash at any moment. Captain Dan and I were loath to cut the line; stirred and roused as we were, it was difficult to give in. We took the chance that as long as our propeller turned the swordfish would not ram us.

But if we had only known what we were soon to learn, we might have spared ourselves further toil and dread.

Suddenly the line began to whiz off the reel. This time the fish took off several hundred feet, then stopped. The line slacked. Dan wound up the slack, and then the fish jerked out more. Still he did not run. I let go of the rod and raised myself to look out into the gloom. I could just make out the pale obscurity of heaving sea, wan and mysterious under the starlight. I heard splashes.

"Listen, Dan," I called. "What do you make of that? He's on the surface."

Captain Dan relaxed a little and listened. Then I heard more splashes, the angry swirl of water violently disturbed, the familiar swishing sound. Then followed a heavy thump. After that soft, light splashes came from the darkness here and there. I heard the rush of light bodies in the air. Then a skittering splash, right near the boat, showed us where a flying fish had ended his flight.

"Dan! Flying fish! All around us—in the air!" I ejaculated.

We listened again, to be rewarded by practically the same sounds. Captain Dan rested the rod on the gunwale, pointing it straight out where we heard the swordfish. *Snap!* Then he wound in the slack line.

"There!" he boomed, as he dropped the rod and waved his big hands. "Do you know what that broadbill is doin' out there? He's feedin' on flyin' fish. He's got hungry an' thought he'd feed up a little. Never knew he was hooked! . . . Eleven hours an' a half—an' he goes to feedin'! . . . By gosh! if that ain't the limit!"

It was long after midnight when we reached the island. Quite a crowd of fishermen and others interested waited for us at the pier, and heard our story with disappointment and wonder. Some of our angler friends made light of the swordfish stunts, especially that one of his chasing flying fish after being fought for more than eleven hours. It did seem strange, improbable. But I had learned that there were stranger possibilities than this in connection with the life and habits of the denizens of the deep. I shall always be positive of the enormous size of this broadbill, and that, after being fought for half a day, and while still hooked, he began chasing flying fish.

IV

XIPHIAS GLADIUS 418 POUNDS

IT took five hours and more of heartbreaking work to catch my 418-pound broadbill swordfish and we did not back up the boat on him when he came threshing to the surface and jab three or four gaffs in him.

I want to tell the exact truth about the taking of this 418-pound broadbill, and see if my readers will not share my idea of the finest and squarest and most thrilling method of catching this magnificent fish.

Much as I have written about old *Xiphias gladius* during the last two years, none of it has gone into print. Broadbill angling is perilously in danger of being ruined, if it is not already ruined. But for the present I must leave such sad truths as that to be told by other anglers.

Nevertheless, as it has long been my ambition and intention to write a narrative and scientific book on *Xiphias gladius*, I want to state that I am doing so, and I mean to tell the truth and to be as accurate as a naturalist-sportsman can be. No book of any kind, fiction or adventure or biology, could make much of a bid for permanence if it did not tell the truth. How can a writer best serve his audience?

Years ago I wrote that to catch fish was not all of fishing. I can say now that the capture of a fish, thrilling and boyhood-recalling as it may be, is the least of the profit which comes to me from roaming the sea. I love the grand old Pacific with its league-long swells, its silver fog banks, its vast sunlit heaving expanse, its mysterious and continuous currents, its life, its beauty and color and movement. There glooms the dark blue sea! The ocean is the mother of life, the maker of rain, the great natural force of the earth.

The beginning of the 1920 season at Avalon found me without a boatman. All the experienced boatmen were engaged for the best months. I made a deal with Captain Sid Boerstler, comparatively a newcomer to the colony. He was an expert engineer, young, strong, willing, but he had not any knowledge of swordfishing. This R. C. and I undertook to teach him. I hope it is not unbecoming to my narrative to mention here that in 1920 and 1921 Captain Sid caught the most swordfish.

He had a boat that he had helped build—a cracker box, some of his facetious rival boatmen called it—and an old automobile engine that gave out the most obnoxious and sickening odor that I ever endured. R. C. and I stood this day after day and week after week, until the ordeal passed into months. Some days it was worse, and on these days we came home sick. We were really suffering from gasoline poisoning, but did not realize that until afterward.

Captain Sid worked over this engine. He lost sleep; he tried out a good many plans; every morning he would beam at us and say: "Got the engine fixed all right. She won't stink any more. You see, the speedometer was refusing to assimilate the gas properly. Then the oil— it was dripping into the carburetor and refused the transmission. This, you see, made the pistons turn round in the cylinders—the wrong way—and so when the spark hit the oil it caught fire and burned. This made the sesquipedalian smell. But it's O.K. now."

R. C. would look skeptically at our genial and intelligent boatman and say: "Sid, you sure know all about engines."

That day the odor would strike us worse than ever. We would come back in a state of coma. Captain Sid would be distracted, and once he really admitted it was a bad smell, and then next morning he would be radiant again.

Moreover, R. C. and I never felt safe in that boat. It was good enough as ordinary motor boats go, but it was far from being invulnerable to a broadbill. We sighted eighty-six broadbills in three months, passed a bait in front of seventy-five of them, got sixteen strikes, had twelve fish hooked, and caught one—my 418 pounder.

R. C. pointed out to me how very easily a gaffed swordfish could make a surge, catch the gaff rope under the propeller, and pull out half the stern of the boat. There are many things a broadbill swordfish can do. Only the anglers who have fished for years for this species have appreciation of the peril.

R. C. and I have had three broadbills threaten to ram us, one of which had thrown the hook. We also had one break the line and circle past our stern so swiftly that we could not believe our eyes. Only the furious boil of the water attested to the speed and proximity of that swordfish. Suppose he had hit us!

Boschen, who introduced fishing for broadbills, told me often of the undoubted danger in the pursuit. Farns-

worth, who is the best boatman ever developed at Catalina, had his boat rammed by a broadbill, and no doubt
he would corroborate my statements. Danielson believes
the broadbill danger is little understood. Adams, who
has caught five broadbills in eight years, will not fight
one after dark, which is the time they get thoroughly
mad.

I believe most of these heavy fish fought by anglers
scarcely know they are hooked. They swim deep and
slow, until the line snaps or wears out. But some of
them know they are hooked. Mine certainly knew it
and he did not let us forget it. To conclude on this point,
R. C. and I believe that the 1920 season was not only
the hardest ordeal we ever endured, but the most dangerous experience of any kind we ever had. Lassoing mountain lions, hunting the grizzly bear, and stalking the
fierce tropical jaguar, former pastimes of ours, are hardly
comparable to the pursuit of *Xiphias gladius*. It takes
more time, patience, endurance, study, skill, nerve, and
strength, not to mention money, of any game known to
me through experience or reading. If it ever has been
mastered, Boschen and Farnsworth are the only angler
and boatman who ever accomplished the feat. Adams
with his five swordfish certainly confesses he has not. I
have caught two in nine years, and have seen more and
hooked more than any angler since Boschen. I have made
a special pursuit and study of *Xiphias gladius*, and
have had a boat built—the *Gladiator*—just for that purpose. And I have only begun to appreciate the strangeness, intelligence, speed, strength, and endurance of this
king of the sea.

In view of these facts, how absurd and unfair for
broadbill swordfishing to be falsely represented all over
the world! To be sure, most fishing is largely a matter
of luck. Anybody can catch almost any kind of a fish

in some unheard-of lucky way. Fluke—the anglers say! But there were never any flukes in broadbill swordfishing. The broadbill is caught either fairly or unfairly.

This great and almost unconquerable fish should have a square deal. How is he going to get a square deal when some boatmen are jealous and most anglers keen to excel? I have not the slightest idea. Is sportsmanship and conservation gaining in this country? No! The good old U. S. is going the way of crass materialism. Will there be any fish for our great-grandchildren? No! Not unless so-called sportsmen band together for conservation.

What is it to catch a broadbill swordfish in a fair battle? To subdue him by dint of your own stalk, skill, strength, and endurance. Boschen's world record 463 pounds was hooked in the heart with two hooks. Boschen was a giant in strength. He managed somehow to hold that fish—to keep him from breaking away—for three strenuous hours, when the fish weakened from loss of blood. That was a fair battle.

Parsons's record swordfish weighed 422. At the end of five hours of terrific and persistent strain Parsons hauled that swordfish close to the boat. Danielson gaffed it. The fish tore a hole in its side and swam away. In another hour of hard work Parsons brought it to the boat again, and they held it. That was a fair battle.

Adams's 377-pound swordfish fought for hours and only gave up when Adams pulled his stomach out. It had swallowed the hook. This was a fair battle.

Danielson and I had a nine-hour battle with a swordfish and lost him. He and R. C. had a eleven-and-one-half-hour fight and lost the fish. My notebooks tell of two seven-hour struggles, three over six hours, two of five, and many under that time—all of which fish were lost. My 260-pound broadbill was hooked in the corner of the mouth and fought six hours exactly. I was sick that night and crippled for days.

There have been innumerable instances of anglers fighting and losing broadbills after long hours. It used to be a joke on the pier. These must all have been fair fights.

But a broadbill gaffed in a few minutes after being hooked—that is not to the credit of the angler. Nor is it a fluke! Nor can it be called good luck! A broadbill that swims to the surface in a half hour or so, to see what is the pesky thing bothering him—to look around—and has a harpoon, or three or four gaffs, jabbed into him is most certainly not caught honestly or fairly.

Every angler is entitled to his own peculiar way of being happy. My way—up to the present—has been to give the fish a square deal, and to try to write that home to less thoughtful anglers. I hope I may be able to stick to my ideal.

On July 19th, of this 1920 season, it chanced that R. C. did not go out with us. There ought always to be three men on a boat, one to hold the rod, the boatman at the wheel, and the third to stand up high and watch the maneuvers of the swordfish when we circle him with a bait.

The morning was ideal. A high fog hung over the island, letting through a diffused sunlight. The sea was a rippling dark blue, with smooth heaving slicks here and there. When the slight breeze blew the odor from the exhaust into my face I was miserable; when it blew the other way I was happy.

We were roaming the sea in search of the sickle-shaped fins of *Xiphias gladius*. This is the most fascinating of all kinds of stalking game. It has to become experience before it can be appreciated. For an hour or two it is pleasant, exhilarating, beautiful. But the wide expanse, the glare of the sky, the light on the water become hard on the eyes. Darkened glasses are necessary. After three or four hours this constant straining becomes painful. After days and weeks it becomes torture. If you are fortunate in finding swordfish frequently the strain is broken and excitement dominates. Time flies! If you see one swordfish a day you are rewarded. If you miss seeing fins for a stretch of eighteen days, as happened to us once, you are to be congratulated if you stick. I do not believe one angler in a thousand can stand even a few days without seeing fish. They go to hunting tuna or Marlin swordfish, or quit. But that is not what Boschen called broadbill swordfishing.

This day we traveled fifteen miles toward San Pedro before we were out of sight of all boats. Alone on the sea! That to me is one of the allurements of this game. We ran for miles farther toward the California shore, then westward, and then farther inshore, until from my perch on the deck I could see the surf break on the rocks.

The sea changed all the time. Yet it seemed empty. No schools of bait, no splashes of fish, no wheeling shearwater ducks, no wakes of sharks, no life of any kind. But that was only a deceit of the deep. The old ocean was full of fish.

At eleven-thirty I sighted fins far ahead, all of a mile. There are times when I can see a swordfish fully two miles. But I have exceptionally keen sight and have had long experience on desert and sea. There are other times when the smooth opal surface of water deceives, blurs, magnifies. Fog, high or low, is conducive to mystery. This swordfish I saw plainly and the old thrill shot over me. I had come to know why the professional swordfishermen of the Atlantic loved this stalk. For it was really stalking big game of the sea.

[127]

We ran down to him and found him to be a large-finned fellow, lazily meandering around. My bait was a fresh barracuda nearly three feet long. We kept far away from the fish, and circling him, tried to drag this bait in front of him. After several attempts we succeeded. But the swordfish turned away from it. We tried again, and yet again. He would not show any interest in our barracuda. This is one of the trying circumstances in fishing for swordfish—so few of them will take a bait. One in every ten is my record! I believe they strike better in the fall. It is tantalizing to hunt all day for a swordfish, and find one—only to have him refuse your lure. At last we drove this fellow down.

About noon, some four or five miles off the California shore, Captain Sid sighted another.

I stood up, holding my rod and letting out my line, and really before we were ready or had begun to circle this fish he gave a flirt of his tail and went under in the direction of my bait. And he hit it hard enough to stagger me. That strike of a swordfish is the most thrilling thing I know of in the angling game. He hit the barracuda with his sword. The blow made my line whip up. I waited, tense and quaking. Never at such moments could I be calm. He hit my bait again. Sid stood beside me, jabbering like a wild man. I did not know what he said. All my sense seemed strained on the wait for the line to begin slipping off my reel. Our quarry struck the bait again, not so hard, and then he swam away with it, slowly and ponderously. Everything was going fine. Then he let go of it. I waited a long time. But he did not take it again.

"There he is," said Sid, tensely, pointing.

And sure enough, our swordfish had come up some distance away.

"We'll let him rest a few moments, then try again," I said, reeling in my bait.

We drifted there, watching him mill on the surface. It occurred to me that he might jump. Broadbills do some strange things. I absolutely believe they will pitch out of the water just to get a look at a boat. I have seen many swordfish do this after we had worked around them for a while. So I got my camera and pointed it in his direction and watched him. Strange to relate, he sank low in the water, and then leaped almost entirely out. It was a spectacle to behold, and I yelled as I clicked my camera on him.

To get a fine photograph of a swordfish was better than killing him. And as his heavy round silver-and-amber body momentarily poised above the surface, my eye caught sight of a huge black remora clinging to him. Then he soused back, and came up again, to show his fins as before.

I was elated. Surely I had snapped my picture just right. Light, time, position could not have been better. And if I had gotten him at all, certainly that remora would show. And if it showed, that would be the finest photograph I had ever taken.

"Sid, did you see that big remora sticking to him?" I asked.

"See nothing! I had buck fever," replied my boatman.

Surely my eyes had not deceived me. Almost positive was I that I had secured a great photograph of this wonderful fish and one of the strange parasites of the deep. The *remora, pilot fish, sucking fish,* and *shipholder* are one and the same. They may differ in size and color, but there is little difference to the unscientific eye. This species has a flat sucker ribbed like a washboard on top of its head and with this it sticks to shark or swordfish, mostly near his gills, from which it sucks blood. I think

I have proved that remoras live inside the gills of Marlin swordfish. I have written elsewhere of this most interesting of parasites, but it will not be amiss to tell of the superstition old-time sailors have for the remora. They call it *shipholder* and claim it attaches itself to the rudder or keel of a ship and retards and sometimes actually stops it. No doubt these ancient mariners still believe this. But it is a fallacy. Powerful as the remora is when he reaches two feet in length, he cannot hold back a ship. The fact that ships have come to a stop at sea is explained by the currentless or dead water in some latitudes. And when at such times sailors have found a remora sticking to their ship they have entertained and spread the strange belief.

Native fishermen in some parts of the world use the remora to catch fish for them—that is to say, they release the remora with line tied to his tail, and let him swim around until he attaches himself to some luckless fish, when they haul him in. The remora does not let go his hold. When the sailors named him *shipholder* there was a good deal of justice, if not strict truth, in its felicitousness.

I recommend the use of the remora to anglers who do not care for the long-drawn and heroic battles with *Xiphias gladius*.

"Let's try him again," suggested Sid. "He took the bait once. Maybe he's hungry."

Assuredly I had the same hope, and meant to try again, but this particular broadbill had been so obliging that I would have thought well of him if he had taken no more notice of us.

The fact was, however, that on the very first turn, he sailed down and hit my bait so hard I was electrified. I had not even been excited. I had really no hope. The sudden shock then was tremendous. Sid yelled, and I shook all over.

It seemed long until the next move of the swordfish, which was to swim off with the barracuda, not slowly this time! He was suspicious. The line flew off my reel. Suddenly he came out on the surface, threshing with his sword, making the water fly. He had felt the hook. Jamming on my drag, I jerked with all my might. The line straightened, came taut, then strung like a wire, and the swordfish made a tremendous lunge. He smashed the green water white and went down in foam. My tight line slipped off the reel. I had hooked that swordfish. How quickly it had happened! It seemed too good to be true.

He went down, down, down so far that I grew frightened and eased the drag. At perhaps five hundred feet he stopped his sounding and swam off up the channel. I pulled as hard as I could, which labor was absolutely futile so far as recovering line was concerned. But Captain Sid manipulated the boat so that eventually I got back half of what had been off the reel.

For perhaps an hour then the swordfish pulled and I pulled, with all the honors in his favor. When a swordfish stayed down deep the battle was nothing but labor. There was no fun, no excitement—nothing but work. That is why so many anglers have said a broadbill fight is no different from that with a shark. They should keep at the game until they hook a few that stay on long enough to get waked up.

Time does not drag in the early stages of a contest with *Xiphias*. I did not hurt myself, but I worked fairly hard. The second hour I warmed up and began to yield to the aggressiveness this species of fish rouses in an angler. I pumped and reeled steadily, encouraged by a gradual drawing of the swordfish closer to the boat. Sometimes he would make a short hard run, then slow up, enabling us to recover the line. But for the most part he stayed down. Naturally I began to feel that I was tiring him out. Perhaps I was. But not so much as he was tiring me out! The battle was unequal. The odds were in his favor. If he kept up that sort of tactics for long the hope of pulling him up, or angering him into furious exertion, was futile. As it was I began to sweat and burn, to have pains in my back. Hands and arms had long been aching.

Captain Sid had his labors also. A hundred times he had thrown that big clutch in and out. And he was always turning the boat. We worked the earlier stages of this battle without much conversation and without excitement. It was a grueling task.

Somewhere around the end of the third hour the swordfish came to the surface and began to bat around with his sword. The sweep of that long black blade was a frightful sight. He was fighting the leader. And while he was thus occupied we might have run down on him and gaffed him. But I wanted to whip him fair or not at all.

We soon made the discovery that he had caught the leader in his tail. It stuck there and placed him at a disadvantage. The wire must have cut deep into the gristle and wedged tight. For he could not dislodge it. This changed his tactics. He plunged halfway out, wagging his head, a huge bird-shaped marine creature with an enormous bill. The wave he made would have done justice to a ferryboat. Then he plunged under to come clear out, high into the air, a marvelous spectacle of white and silver and bronze, a furious fish with staring black eye, slapping gills, waving sword, and magnifi-

Z. G. Scanning the Sea for Fins

Plate xxxiii

Leaping Broadbill Swordfish. This Is the Greatest Marine Photograph I Ever Took. Note the Remora (Sucking Fish or Pilot Fish) Hanging to Swordfish

Plate xxxiv

cent body instinct with ferocity. He splashed down and began to roll.

Here I worked my hardest. I pulled with all my might. I had him tired, and twisted. He could not get headway, or did not try to. The powerful strain I put on the line would not have amounted to much if it had not been that the leader was caught in his tail. With the hook in his mouth, as I thought then, and the end of the leader fast to his tail, I had him sort of "hog-tied," as the cowboys say. I recognized this fact and I did not spare myself in the least. And I began to drag him closer and closer toward the boat.

That strenuous period might have been long or short, I could not tell, and Captain Sid was beyond remembering anything, but the fact was I pumped and reeled the swordfish close enough to prick him with a gaff. Sid just missed getting the gaff in him. The swordfish made such a sudden and tremendous splash that I was heartily glad Sid had missed him.

Then wild as a wild horse he raced away on the surface, making the water fly like a motor boat. Sid's boat answered the helm quickly and it was fast. He got after him before he had all the line out, and we chased him to get it back. From that time the fight grew thrilling and spectacular.

We chased this swordfish all over the ocean—miles and miles, I was certain. He never sounded once. Most of the time we could see his fins, and always the wake he made. And all the time I kept a heavy strain on him. He did not run straight. He ran off at right angles, and often turned to cross ahead or behind us. It took manipulating of rod and boat to keep a tight line. Somehow, except in a few instances, we accomplished it. The leader was still fouled in his tail and he was plainly wild and bewildered. There did not seem to be the slightest indication that he was tired now.

The time came when he doubled back on his trail, to head straight for us. This was embarrassing by reason of the difficulty in reeling up slack line, and disconcerting because I feared he might ram us. Twice I had Sid run out of his path. The third time, however, when the swordfish sheered toward us, I grew curious or brave or angry, and yelled for Sid to let him come. Meanwhile I wound the reel as fast as I could. Once I actually saw the line come up over his tail, over his body and dorsal fin as he faced us.

That swordfish came to the boat, and swam with us, a little astern and perhaps fifteen feet out. I reeled in until my line was tight. And I stood up. I could not help it; that was an instinctive action. I have been cramped in that fishing chair more than once when a swordfish got too close.

What a fearful and beautiful fish! He seemed tawny in color, short, round, not large at all. Only his naked sword and his black eye looked vicious. He swam with us. I watched him perhaps for ten seconds, and I lost my fear of him. It did not occur to me then that but for the revolving propeller he might have hit us. Why do these swordfish ram ships at sea? It is a common occurrence. The English marine log is full of such recordings. I could see where the leader, clear to the ring, was fast in his tail. But I could not see where it went into his mouth. It was on the other side. Even then I grasped something queer about this.

"Sid, he's a little fish—not over two hundred," I cried as I jammed my rod back in the socket and crowded into the seat. "Let's see."

And I exerted myself to the utmost to haul the sword-

TOWARD THE END OF THE BATTLE

PLATE XXXV

Xiphias gladius, 418 Pounds

Plate xxxvi

fish closer. Then I saw he was tired. I rolled him over. But with a fling of his tail that deluged us he plunged away. We followed him, and very soon he did precisely the same thing as before. He came up to us, and when I shut down with all my might on the reel I almost held him.

"We're going to get him," I yelled. What prompted such assumption I could not guess, but I felt it. Captain Sid made wild and whirling use of words.

Before long the swordfish changed his course and eventually came alongside. I had released the strain and did not put it on until he got close. He was certainly growing logy. That renewed my strength and I bent the rod double and cracked my back. Probably I dragged that swordfish a matter of six feet, but I could not have dragged him an inch farther to save my life.

But Sid reached him with a gaff. The ocean seemed to explode. I saw a cloud of spray come aboard. And in it Sid appeared, making frantic movements. He all but went overboard. The gaff rope, after it tore out of his hands, had caught one of his legs. He had a narrow escape.

Our *Xiphias* went roaring away, dragging the gaff and rope. We saw both plainly. My line paid steadily off the reel.

"Say—I got him—high up—near his head!" panted Sid. "What was it—happened?"

"Grab your wheel. He's our fish," I said, grimly.

Then as we set off again after this eagle of the sea we saw a war vessel, a mine sweeper, come bearing down on us, too close for comfort. Sid waved frantically. It soon developed that the officers on that boat saw what we were doing, and they hove to and watched us through their glasses while the swordfish stayed in their vicinity.

He remained on the surface, but did not turn again. I had Sid run up on him until we were within a hundred feet. Then I put all the muscle I had left into the task of stopping him. That muscle, after five hours, was not very much. Nevertheless, it told. He slowed; he rolled; he wearily wagged his great tail. Also he gradually settled in the water, until his fins went under and I could see only his color.

All of a sudden he pitched up, head out, and plunged sullenly, to go down, until he was heading straight. Down, down, down! I watched the line slip off. I knew what that sounding meant. He was a spent fish. But I must stop him or lose him. The fact was I could not stop him. At one thousand feet depth he stopped of his own accord, and there he hung. He never made another move.

I could not budge him an inch, but by holding my reel and having Sid run the boat very gently forward I got him coming. He was a dead weight and every second I looked to see the line snap. But it held. And ever so slowly I reeled it in, inch by inch. Probably I never worked so hard, in that condition, in my life before. It took half an hour to get him where I could gain any line worth considering. But at last I had him coming up.

Sid nearly fell overboard, looking down to try to find him. When he did see him he let out a stentorian roar.

The swordfish came up tail first, dead. We did not need to gaff him again, but of course we did. I was so exhausted and my hands hurt so that I was of little help to Sid in trying to haul him aboard. We could not lift even his tail out of the water, and we had to tow him back to Avalon. All during that three-hour ride back the swordfish grew larger and larger in my sight.

When he was hauled up on the dock I found the hook fast in his body on the right side. The leader passed between his jaws and down his left side and was embedded in his tail. He had never been hooked in the mouth at all. The ring on my leader must have caught in his tail the very first plunge. If it had loosened I would have lost my swordfish that instant. Four hundred and eighteen pounds!

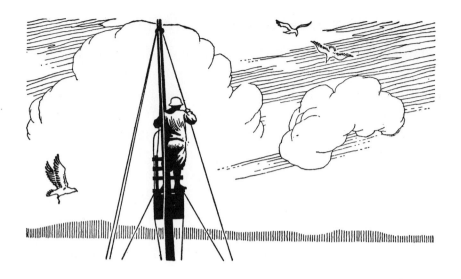

V

WOLVES OF THE SEA

ONE day last August at Catalina Island a well-known boatman, Yellowtail John, came in with a wild and wonderful tale about fishes. It so happens that Yellowtail John is noted for remarkable fish stories centering around himself and his boat *Dragon*. But John, owing to a most fertile imagination and invention, was seldom believed by his comrade boatmen, and then only when he could substantiate his claims by facts.

The particular story in question was the most lurid and incredible ever related by Yellowtail John; and certainly would have been scouted by everybody had it not been for the fact that I upheld John, and was in turn upheld by my brother R. C. and by Lone Angler Wiborn, and in a measure by Adams and Bandini.

Here, in somewhat condensed form, follows Yellowtail John's story.

"Blackfish—killer whales—dem dam' orcas, un' t'ousands un' t'ousands of 'em! I seen 'em. I was all surrounded by 'em. Un' you joost waid un' when Zane Grey comes in—he tells you some fish story, I bet you five t'ousand dollars.

"Such a sight I never see for my whole life. Un' t'ousands of blackfish chasin' porpoises un' bonito shark, un' Marlin, un' doony [tuna] un' de broadbill swordfish. Un' right in de middle is Zane Grey, on his boat *Gladiator*, havin' a time for his life. Mit a big gun he shoots, un' he shoots some more, but shootin' didn't hurt dem dam' orcas. Loog here now, I'm dolin' you what I never see before of my whole life. I seen orcas chasin' fish all over, un' some jumb oud. Un' bonito shark was tore to bieces right by my boat. Un' den a big broadbill swordfish jumbs oud high. He would of weighed six hundred pounds. Un' after him jumbs a blackfish twice as big—un' catches him by de tail. Un' dey come down mit awful splash, all white un' red, un' dat broadbill goes in bites. I'm got a forty-forty rifle, un' I'm take some shots. Un' look here I'm shoot dat big blackfish through de back, un' makes him mad like hell, un' I'm dolin' you me un' de *Dragon* beat it. Joost you waid un' when Zane Grey comes in he tells you some fish story."

I am herewith recording that Yellowtail John was assuredly right in his concluding words. I cannot, however, substantiate John in all that he claimed he saw. For instance, he said he saw me shooting with a rifle. As a matter of fact this was wholly unfounded. Neither R. C. nor Lone Angler nor I used anything but a camera. Our opportunity was too wonderful to admit any thought, save for pictures. Another angle which shows John's degree of excitement and exaggeration is the fact that my boat *Gladiator* was never within half a mile of John's *Dragon*. When we ran down upon this mêlée of blackfish, Yellowtail John was already retreating. It is my opinion that John witnessed the first and therefore the best and most marvelous part of this performance. I believe that he actually saw orcas kill shark and swordfish. Judging from what we experienced, it is not difficult to believe, incredible as it may seem. *Xiphias gladius*, the great broadbill swordfish, is surely the king, the lion of the sea. But nevertheless, he could not prevail against even a few of these wolfish orcas.

Perhaps in ten years of deep-sea angling I have seen fifty schools of these orcas or blackfish or whale killers. I cannot be absolutely sure, but I believe I saw one school in the Gulf Stream off Long Key, Florida. The fish were black and too large for porpoises. But I could not get close enough positively to identify them. All the others were located in the Pacific. During the summer season at Catalina it is no unusual thing to see a dozen schools. The Avalon boatmen certainly give these blackfish a black name, though I could never find any proof of its justification. But the boatmen were afraid of blackfish and did not like to stay in their vicinity.

For my part I had always believed the orcas shy and wild. Certainly they always sounded at the approach of a boat, and seldom came to the surface again short of half a mile. Some of the schools extended over miles of sea, and must have numbered thousands of fish. At a distance the orca somewhat resembles a porpoise. He comes up with the same motion and has a sharp dorsal fin. On closer view, however, the orca is black, and has a blunt nose, like a battering ram, and a huge sharp spiked dorsal. Porpoises are brown or mottled gray. Like a whale, the orca spouts from a blowhole, and the "blow" can be heard at some distance. The puff of white spray, like steam, can be seen for a mile. It is, of course, very much smaller than that made by a whale.

In size the orca appears to vary, according to my observations, from fifteen feet in length to thirty or more. I do not hesitate to record that I watched five orcas for half an hour from the deck of the *Cabrillo* and not one of them appeared under thirty feet in length, and certainly would have weighed half a dozen tons. As they lunged out of the water I could see the blunt head, and the white marking of the under part of body. These, however, were exceptions in size. In August, 1921, R. C. and I noted several large orcas leaping clear of the water. We could not get close. These incidents of the sea are rare. Like other phenomena of the deep, they must be waited and watched for.

Five years ago, one morning, I perceived, far out at sea, a tremendous white maelstrom. Spouts of water shot as high as those made by the great guns of the warships at practice. Dark leaping forms appeared against the background of threshing white. I had no doubt a whale had been attacked by orcas. This is a spectacle second only to the rare and terrible fight between swordfish and whale.

In consulting the Encyclopædia Britannica, I find that the best description of the fish I am writing about comes under the name Grampus (*Orca gladiator*), a cetacean belonging to the *Delphinidæ* or dolphin family. It is characterized by rounded head, large conical teeth, and high dorsal fin. The upper parts are nearly uniform glossy black, and the under parts white, with a strip of white over each eye. The Old French word was *grapois*, *graspeis*, or *craspeis*, from Mediæval Latin *crassus piscis*, fat fish. This was adapted into English as *grapeys*, *graspeys*, and in the sixteenth century becomes *graunde pose*. The final corruption to "grampus" appears in the eighteenth century, and was probably nautical in origin. The animal is also known as the "killer," in allusion to its ferocity in attacking its prey, which consists largely of seals, porpoises, and the smaller dolphins. Its fierceness is only equaled by its voracity, which is such that in a specimen measuring twenty-one feet in length the remains of thirteen seals and thirteen porpoises were found, in a more or less digested state. The grampus appeared to have choked in an endeavor to swallow another seal, the skin of which was found entangled in its teeth. These cetaceans hunt in packs or schools, and commit great havoc among the white whales, which occasionally plunge ashore to escape their persecutors. The grampus is an inhabitant of northern seas, occurring on the shores of Greenland. It has been caught as far south as the Mediterranean.

I have no doubt that the grampus is the identical blackfish frequently found in Catalina waters. In September of this year I saw blackfish off the mouth of Campbell River, Vancouver Island, British Columbia. The Indians told me these fish were common in the straits there. I recognized them as the same I have watched off the California coast.

But it is important to mention that though orca, grampus, killer whale, and blackfish all belong to the same species, there are essential differences, only a few of which can be recorded here.

The orcas, like the whales, dolphins, porpoises, etc., are all true mammals, with warm blood, and they suckle their young. The tail of this species is in singular contrast to that of other fishes, having a pair of lateral pointed expansions called flukes, forming a horizontal triangular propelling organ. The need of this species to come often to the surface to breathe is what developed the horizontal flukes. That is to say, the upward and downward movements necessary caused the tail to expand horizontally. A popular idea connected with this species, especially with whales, is that they take water in at the mouth and spout it through the blowhole. This

ORCA ATTACKING WHALE

PLATE XXXVII

The Hammerhead Shark

Plate xxxviii

is erroneous. The blowhole is a nostril, situated on the highest part of the head, and is for respiration. Whales and their kind do not spout water, but a vapor condensed in their lungs. Sometimes, of course, this blow sends up water that flows over the animal's head.

This species has very small eyes and does not see well. Nor is the sense of smell highly organized. Mostly they depend upon hearing when below the surface.

In the grampus, *Orca gladiator*, the teeth form about twenty pairs, above and below, and are very large and stout. In the lesser killer whale, *Pseudorca crassidens*, the teeth are confined to the anterior half of rostrum and part of lower jaw, and are small, conical, curved and sharp. In the ca'ing whale, or blackfish (*Globicephalus melas*), there are about ten pairs of upper and lower teeth. Many other differentiations have been recorded, most of which are discernible only to scientists.

Only one of this family, the orca I am describing, eats other warm-blooded animals, such as seals and porpoises and members of its own species.

Allen, of the California Biological Service, states that "whales are evidently pursued mainly for their tongues, although the killers do not scruple to bite off chunks of fin or flesh."

Roy Chapman Andrews has found that "in trying to get the tongue several orcas have been seen to attack a whale, while one or more at a time thrust snouts between the whale's lips in an effort to force his mouth open. Such vicious attacks upon full-grown whales indicate the probability that great numbers are killed while still very young."

Dr. Hanna of the California Academy of Sciences gave an estimate that orcas destroy each year more than $1,000,000 worth of seals.

The day of my never-to-be-forgotten experience with the orcas occurred about the middle of August. As was our wont when roaming the sea for broadbill swordfish, we had headed north along the steamer course, and were probably near the middle of the channel when I sighted blackfish. There appeared to be rather a large number of them and more concentrated than usual. Also I saw a goodly number of shearwater ducks flying around, and this caused me to run the *Gladiator* off her course. We are always keen to investigate the actions of those queer ducks.

Ahead of us one boat was in sight, closer to the blackfish, and some distance to the westward. Behind, a couple of miles or more, came Adams and Bandini in the boat *Angler*. When we changed our course, which had been due north from them, they held on as before. No other boats were in sight.

R. C. and Wiborn were with me this day, a most fortunate circumstance; and when I called them they quickly shared my curiosity as to the blackfish. I sent R. C. aloft to the lookout chair, while Wiborn and I watched from the deck. Captain Sid emerged from the cabin, and together we bent keen eyes ahead.

I soon made out big splashes on the surface and black shapes clearing the water, and after studying them for a moment I knew some kind of extraordinary action was taking place.

"Speed up, Cap," I said to Sid. "That mess ahead looks queer to me." Then I called up to R. C. "Use your eyes now. Like as not this is one of the chances to see something."

"Big porpoises rarin' around," was R. C.'s dubious observation.

The sea was calm, smooth as glass, with great long low heaving swells. And its wonderful open surface showed

THE THRESHER SHARK. NOTE TAIL WITH WHICH HE KILLS HIS PREY

PLATE XXXIX

THE "GLADIATOR" AT CLEMENTE ISLAND

PLATE XL

only one roughened spot, which was the white water ahead. The *Gladiator*, speeding at ten knots, would soon enlarge our view of this spectacle, whatever it was. Captain Sid was the first to see that the boat ahead was Yellowtail John's *Dragon* and it had turned away from the blackfish.

"Johnnie's runnin' the wheels off his boat," said Sid.

Wiborn next made the observation that Adams and Bandini had turned the *Angler* to follow us. But I paid no attention to these boats. Before we were within a half mile of the blackfish I called R. C. down out of the crow's nest and ordered everybody to get ready with cameras.

We passed the *Dragon* perhaps half a mile to the westward. Sid said there was excitement aboard that boat, but I did not look. I was intent on the blackfish. The mass of them appeared to have concentrated in one area, perhaps a space of fifty acres, and here they were breaking the water white, puffing clouds of spray, bobbing up with their sharp black fins. Shearwater ducks were everywhere, not in large flocks, but scattered all over this area, and from their actions I knew they were feeding.

We were swiftly bearing down upon this animated scene, and various indeed were the comments made by my comrades.

"Porpoises rounded up a school of bait. I see the ducks feeding," ventured R. C.

The idea of the shearwaters picking up crippled anchovies, as they do when hovering near a school of feeding tuna, had naturally come to me also, but I soon rejected it. Still, on the moment I could not reason out why, nor explain what the ducks were feeding on. I watched and waited.

"Say, there's somethin' doin'," yelled Sid, as if he had made a discovery all by himself.

Wiborn's shrewd observation was that the porpoises showing were either very lazy or very tired. Now I had never seen either a lazy or a tired porpoise. And that realization put a keen edge on my growing curiosity. When we were within a few hundred yards of the turbulent black and white water I called for Sid to slow down the boat and stay at the wheel. Soon it appeared we were right upon the mass of blackfish, and that stragglers had begun to show on each side of us and behind.

It was such a big scene that it could not be grasped in its entirety, and to watch one blackfish or a few of them seemed impossible. But that is what should have been done. All around us could be heard the whistle and puff of blackfish as they came up to "blow." But these blowing fish did not make the quick angry surges and splashes on the surface. The main line of blackfish appeared ahead and were raising what might be termed a wall of white water before them. Out of this advancing foamy line porpoises were leaping. Yet their movements could scarcely be so designated. It seemed a slow labored surge. On the moment I did not connect this action with the pursuing blackfish nor did I think of the porpoises as trying to escape an enemy.

We reached that wall of white water and glided through it, and spread it so we were surrounded. I could not explain, yet I saw that the action changed. But neither ducks nor blackfish nor porpoises showed the slightest fear of the *Gladiator*. Naturally I had expected the fish to go down and disappear. But they did not. They swarmed around the boat. Porpoises, dozens of them, swam close before the bow and they stayed there, just swooping up to show their mottled backs. I saw scars on their gray sides. Then a long purple shape of a blackfish would glide in on one of the porpoises. Down he would point his nose and sound with one tired

BLACKFISH AND ORCA, WOLVES OF THE SEA (Plates xli to liv)

PLATE XLI

PLATE XLII

PLATE XLIII

PLATE XLIV

PLATE XLV

PLATE XLVI

PLATE XLVII

PLATE XLVIII

PLATE XLIX

PLATE L

PLATE LI

PLATE LII

PLATE LIII

PLATE LIV

sweep of his flukes, and the huge purple shape would sound with him. I saw this action several times. The great blackfish swam alongside and under us, sometimes a slow gliding shape and again a purple flash, as swift as lightning. I tried to look in every direction, in order not to miss anything, and as a result I did not concentrate on a few fish and actions close at hand. Presently, however, I saw a shearwater duck holding and trying to swallow a good-sized piece of raw flesh. Next I perceived a dark spreading shadow in the green water. It seemed red. It disintegrated or mixed with the water. Blood! All in a flash then I understood this scene. The orcas, or blackfish, had rounded up a school of porpoises and had chased them until they had become so exhausted they could scarcely swim. Certainly they did not show any of their wonderful speed. Nor did they sound like a plummet. They just dove, wearily, a dead weight, and assuredly when they went down they never came up. On the other hand the blackfish moved with marvelous swiftness and power.

What more I might have learned from this scene of nature's incomprehensible ruthlessness never transpired. For suddenly an enormous orca, all of twenty-five feet in length and correspondingly huge of bulk, leaped high in the air, and turning clear over he dove back head first, to cut the water like a spear. Involuntarily we all yelled in amaze, awe, and admiration. Then I awoke to our singular opportunity.

"CAMERAS!" I shouted, at the top of my lungs.

Then, as if the leap of the huge orca and my cry were signals, these monsters of the deep began to play around us, to come out full length, to slide up and up into the sunlight all wet and shiny and leathery, dark graceful forms, instinct with life. What wonderful moments! If I had not been so passionately bent on photographing these leaping orcas! But I was in such a frenzied hurry to procure snapshots that I really did not see what I might have seen. As for my comrades, they were as spellbound or frenzied as I was. Captain Sid would turn the wheel so as to keep the boat in the thick of the mêlée; then he too would point his camera, trying to catch a blackfish in the air. Wiborn danced around on the deck like an Indian. R. C. nearly fell off the bow, and as for myself, I was utterly unable to grasp the magnificent opportunity. It seemed I could not catch an orca at the right second. I was too slow, too excited, too overwhelmed. I wanted to snap pictures and see at the same time. I was in too great a hurry.

Once the grandfather of all these orcas leaped fully as high as the mast of the *Gladiator*. All the boys except me had just snapped their cameras. I was waiting for just this chance. He came out, slowly it seemed, and wagged upward with incredible grace and ease. Not fifty feet from the boat! He would have weighed tons. His white glistening under side faced me, beautiful as the silver of a tarpon. He came up without splashing any water. Up he towered. I was ready, strung with intense eagerness, yet I could not, did not snap my camera. I was paralyzed. It seemed too great a picture for me. That wild and wagging shape, so close I plainly smelled the fishy odor, was too much for my senses. High up in the air this orca turned over and went down head first, black as coal against the sky, and he plunged into the sea with thundering crash. Then I heard the wild exultant yells of my comrades. They believed I had secured another great photograph. But I had failed. Failed just because the size and beauty and power of that sea monster had paralyzed me! An instant afterward another orca, half as large, leaped twenty feet into the air, and I caught him with the camera as he turned.

After that I steadied somewhat, and with clearer gaze and collected wits I waited for more exceptional chances. We had found that in photographing leaping fish, even with four or five cameras working, there always came a magnificent leap after everybody had snapped. I waited for this and had some temptations hard to resist.

I saw Wiborn photograph a blackfish in a straight greyhound forward leap that was exceedingly beautiful and wonderful to watch. This fellow was a big one and a forty-foot leap appeared nothing to him. A knife blade could not have cut the water more keenly. This fish, like some of the others, seemed to be leaping for our edification. They were playing around us, giving us exhibitions of their prowess.

R. C. stood at the bow of the boat, and I have seen him less strung when shooting at a grizzly bear. This was the kind of hunting we cared most for and which gave us the keenest thrills. I saw R. C. photograph one orca that was plunging ahead of the boat. The flukes of his tail appeared five feet across. R. C.'s exultant yell pealed out, and a second later, when he snapped two orcas in the air at once, he roared with stentorian lungs. What fun we were having! To see wild creatures in their haunts, to watch them, and capture something of their beauty and action, and all without harm to them— that is the ideal achievement for the lover of nature.

Just after R. C. performed his triumphant feat of photographing the two blackfish I was attracted by Wiborn's yell, and wheeling I was just in time to see the end of what must have been an extraordinary leap of another fish. So holding my camera tight against my body, I watched the boiling water where he had gone down. We had begun to learn how very often these fish leaped twice.

Suddenly, like a huge black bat, out he came, slick,

noiseless as oil, marvelously propelled, to shoot high into the air. He was far from the boat, but I saw him distinctly, two thousand pounds of black muscle, it seemed, and assuredly a sight to remain forever in a fisherman's memory. He shot up until I held my breath. Indeed, he resembled a prehistoric bird of exceeding proportions, and as he turned over he seemed to assume the shape of a colossal duck. In this position I photographed him, and felt a little recompensed for my loss of the greatest opportunity. No diver ever slipped into the sea more easily, with any less commotion, than that orca.

This appeared to be the last of the high and lofty tumbling. Yet the orcas stayed on the surface, rolling and plunging, banding together in groups, and showing singly. Many purple shadows hovered deep down, moving with the boat.

Some one yelled for me to watch the other boat. Thus I became aware of the presence of Adams and Bandini close at hand on the *Angler*. They were surrounded by rolling blackfish. Adams stood in the stern, reaching as far out as he could with a long gaff, and he was trying his best to hook one of the blackfish.

"He'll get yanked overboard," was R. C.'s terse remark.

"It will be funny if Harry gaffs one. Let's hang around to see what becomes of him," said Wiborn.

But close as the orcas were and many as were Adams's attempts to reach one, he did not succeed in doing so. Fortunate, probably, for both fish and man! I amused myself snapping some pictures of the famous Tuna Club angler trying to gaff a blackfish. While I was doing this there was one huge black old bull of an orca that stuck his head out of the water not far from me. He resembled a black submarine. The white fringe of water round his head looked like teeth, and altogether he presented a formidable picture. I would not have cared to fall over-board in front of him.

Probably we spent an hour among these strange fish. Gradually they quieted down, and left us to go plowing away across the seas, no doubt in search of more prey.

In some faint measure this portrayal of our experience may give an impression of the fascination and mystery of the sea. Never before had I seen the like, and never expect to see it again. This was tragedy, yet scarcely to the superficial eye. It was all beauty and activity and life. The gruesome truth hid under the surface of the ocean. What measureless infinite conflict must go on eternally beneath the waves! Contending tides mean vastly more than the influence of the moon upon the deep. Three-fourths of the earth is covered by salt water. Myriads of creatures lived and strove and died in those boundless blue depths ages before man evolved on the land. Years of observation and thought are necessary to acquire an idea of the tremendousness of the ocean, its staggering fecundity and fertility, its matchless beauty and its various moods, and a profound sense of its inscrutable secrecy.

VI

WHALES' TAILS

THIS morning did not look propitious. It was rather light, with wide spaces of clear sky, and a ripply sea. The wind was chill. We decided to run to Catalina Harbor. I wrote five pages, and did not notice the sea, but it seemed rough. Another bad day! Nevertheless, we went on. When I got through my work a high sea was running from the west and the wind was brisk.

We ran into Catalina Harbor, round the point, the first time for me. I found the bottle-necked landlocked bay very isolated and beautiful. The stone breakwater made by Indians of prehistoric times was exceedingly interesting, as was also the old Chinese pirate ship, the *Ning Po*, resting on the mud, and now a Mecca for sight-seers.

When we ran out to sea again the wind had lulled, the sun had come out, the sea had changed from gray to blue, and as if by magic the fishing day was beautiful. I climbed to the crow's nest. Far out I saw a whale make white water, then sound. I directed captain to head out.

We found two California gray whales feeding out there, and a rare opportunity for pictures appeared at hand. We followed the larger one, a huge gray mottled leviathan of the deep, upward of eighty feet in length. It was most thrilling to approach him. As I had tried this many times before, I did not anticipate much luck. But you never can tell! This old fellow very obligingly stayed up until we got within two hundred feet; then he curved his leathery shining back and doubled his tail into a round knot. Then wondrously rose the wide flukes! I was in a rapture of excitement. And I missed that chance for a picture because a strap had caught on a lever of my camera. The old hoodoo was working! I was sick. But R. C. assured me that he had caught the picture, and that assuaged my discomfiture.

We ran over to the second whale, and followed him to no avail, for he would not lift his flukes. Then when the first one rose again, blowing his white vapor high, we sailed down on him. The very same opportunity presented again, and this time I seized it. I was elated. R. C. and Sid both snapped their cameras at my yell.

We waited for him to come up again, and he was not long in doing so. This circumstance was interesting. I concluded the whale was feeding on the small bait fish numerous just off the harbor. He would go down and make a foray, then rise to breathe. Anyway, we profited marvelously by whatever actuated him to such an unusual proceeding. For ten years I have been trying to take a good picture of a whale sounding with his flukes high in the air.

The next time I was less excited and therefore capable of keen observation. We ran behind him, very slowly and cautiously, and when some two hundred feet away threw out the clutch and drifted. He was wallowing slowly. Sometimes for moments he was still, except for the heave of the sea. He lay there like a wide round gray island beset by tiny waves. Then he would move forward and wag the hindermost part of his enormous body. When he submerged we could follow him by the pale green shadow in the water. It would turn to gray. Then the enormous bulk would rise. Roar! He blew like a foghorn. The white vapor rose high. We saw his blowhole distinctly. It widened after he blew and opened, evidently to inhale. Then his long back slid forward. It appeared he had no dorsal fin. But presently that hove in sight. Next the narrowing body doubled and lifted. How mobile and elastic! He moved as easily and gracefully as a snake. It was fascinating to watch. Behind trailed the wide forked flukes, a beautiful phosphorescent silver green under the water. He made three of these slow surges, puffing each time, and doubling more each time; and on the fourth we yelled in our expectancy. The great tail swooped up very ponderously and so slowly that it was most tantalizing. The sharp edge pointed toward us; the bend of the tail slowly straightened. Up and up heaved the flukes, and a white waterfall poured down upon the sea. Then the vast shiny gray-brown fish tail rose above the horizon, high and wide against the sky and on that supreme instant I yelled for the cameras to shoot. How easily and slowly the flukes slid down into the ocean! The most beautiful sight afforded by marine creatures had been wonderfully presented to us.

We followed this whale five more times, and each time he sounded for us with his magnificent tail in the air. It was an unbelievable good fortune—a reward of constant and persistent work under unfavorable conditions

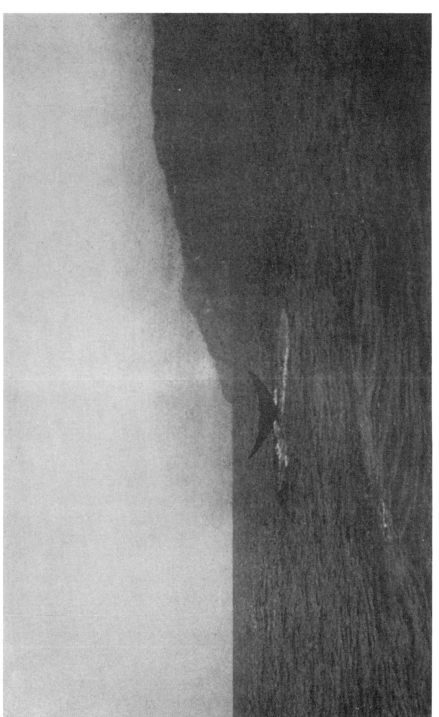

WHALE'S TAILS (Plates lv to lx)
(*The most beautiful sight the sea affords.*)
PLATE LV

PLATE LVI

PLATE LVII

PLATE LVIII

PLATE LIX

PLATE LX

—a proof of the truth of nature. Watching and waiting are all that are needed. The reward is sure.

To me this incident was significant of the wonder of the deep. Out of the blue depths had come the greatest of mammals, centuries old perhaps, to thrill us with the mystery and joy of life.

VII

HERCULEAN ANGLING

BROADBILL-SWORDFISH angling as an art and a labor of Hercules has begun to change only since it was introduced by William Boschen ten years ago. This art as developed by him takes no account of lucky flukes and accidents in the capture of the gladiator of the sea. To find and stalk old *Xiphias gladius*, to induce him to look at a bait, to hook him when he does not strike, and to fight him hour after hour until he is beaten by strength and endurance—this has become recognized as the supreme test of an angler.

On July 21, 1923, an Avalon boat captured a broadbill swordfish weighing 474 pounds. It took the bait and was hooked. It tangled its tail in the airplane-wire leader, rendering it practically helpless. Presently it sounded and died. To the few anglers who had toiled and undergone hardships for years this phenomenal fluke was a disheartening experience. No fisherman who had given months and months to the glaring sea, hunting for these elusive swordfish, hooking only one out of fifty seen, and losing the big ones, could fail to be affected.

This record swordfish was the fifth one in two years that had been lassoed and strangled in these airplane-wire leaders. Three of these tangled their tails and died; one of them cut his throat; and another sawed himself nearly in twain. All of them were captured quickly without fight or use of gaffs.

The remarkable wire leader, lately introduced at Avalon, is thin and pliable as a cord, and unbreakable and unkinkable. If it loops round a swordfish it sticks and cuts deeper and deeper. It is an infernal thing. We have used this leader, along with all the other anglers, but we have never yet entangled a swordfish in it. I imagine that the chances are greatly against doing so. Let any angler go out deliberately to catch a broadbill by fouling him in such a leader and he will find it impossible. What is so confounding relative to this airplane-leader fluke is the conviction we entertained for years that the broadbill swordfish was the one fish in the world which could not be caught through luck.

For three years of our early experiences at Avalon, R. C. would never pass a bait to a broadbill. He became the most expert and successful of Marlin fishermen, but evinced no interest in the great flat-billed swordfish. At that time we did not go out to hunt for broadbills; if we happened to run across one I could not resist dropping him a bait. I think R. C. had an uncanny inkling of what it would take to catch a broadbill. As for me, these great fish always fascinated me. At length I started out for broadbills and it took several summers of hard going to catch my first one—260 pounds.

This experience opened my eyes to a realization of one of the greatest sports known to an angler. The extreme difficulties began slowly to dawn upon me, until I saw the game in all its possibilities. From that time broadbill-swordfishing grew upon me. I persuaded R. C. against his own pleasure to accompany me, and take turn for turn at the rod. I was three more summers in catching my second broadbill.

During these years R. C. hooked a number of broadbills, among them the monster that fought us for eleven and a half hours. R. C. had several other long battles. Gradually he awoke to the greatness of the swordfish and the incomparable fascination of its pursuit. This was much harder for him to realize than it had been for me. For I love the sea and no hour on it is lacking in something of beauty or inspiration. But R. C. was at first no sailor; he suffered from seasickness; it took years for him to become accustomed to rough water. Nevertheless, more from loyalty to me than from inclination, he stuck it out until the magnitude of the game won him.

Then he determined to catch a broadbill for himself. It took him three months of every summer for five years, fifteen months in all. During 1921, 1922, and half of the summer of 1923, I seldom took the rod to try for a swordfish. I didn't want R. C. to miss a chance. Often we quarreled about this. A few times he stayed ashore for a day, hoping I would fish. It was on one of his off days that I caught my 418-pound broadbill.

It seems needful to say here, though I have written it elsewhere, that the hooking and fighting of a broadbill are sheer joy and thrilling excitement. The laborious part of the game comes before that. The pursuit, that is to say, the hunting and stalking of swordfish on the ocean, is not so easy and attractive as one might imagine. In fact, it can become terrible strain. We ran the *Gladiator* from fifty to a hundred miles a day, and always one of us was on the lookout. On hot calm days, with high diffused fog, we were almost sure to sight one or more broadbills. But such days were rare last summer. We had westerly winds, rising early, almost every day. Still we went on.

There were times when I went blind in the crow's nest, peering out over the shining sea, looking for the telltale fins of a broadbill. Owing to my keen sight, largely developed on the desert, I could spot swordfish more easily than the others. R. C. grew to be pretty good. Sid Boerstler, my boatman, could be relied on to sight fins close to the boat. This summer of 1923 I also had Thad Williams, a Florida boatman and old mackerel fisherman, and as I had expected, he was keen to sight fish on the surface. Among us all we did not miss many swordfish.

Besides the strain on the eyes there was the everlasting roll of the *Gladiator*, which "rolled to larboard, rolled to starboard," the hours without exercise, the interminable winds cutting the face, the hot sun or the cold fog, and always the restraint, the wait, the expectation. Sometimes we did not see a swordfish for ten days. Once we went fourteen days—two weeks! This was nothing less than torture.

But still worse, more tantalizing and insupportable, was the fact that after long and patient hunting, when we did find a swordfish, he would not look at the bait. Our average was that about one fish out of twelve would bite. But it seemed vastly more than that. Once we worked thirty-five swordfish without a strike. How interminable the long wait! How hope became a mockery! Then, staggering and exhilarating shock, the thirty-sixth swordfish charged the bait with a rush.

In ninety-three days we sighted 140 swordfish, got a bait to 94, and had 11 strikes. In four of these strikes, however, the swordfish hit the bait and refused to take it. One of the interesting and significant features of this record is the fact that 46 of the 140 swordfish were too wary for us to get a bait near them.

On July 23rd I was up at five o'clock, and found it to be a warm muggy morning, rather dark—the promise of a fine day to hunt swordfish. As good days had been rare, we were keen to go. Every morning we had hopes. They spring eternal in the fisherman's breast. There was a light fog over the island and rather heavy banks out at sea. A long silver line of sunlight ran along the horizon. Like a vast river the sea glided on, gray as the fog in places, burnished brightly when the sunshine filtered through.

At seven o'clock we were off in the *Gladiator*, this morning, for the first time, towing the *Little Gladiator*. The boys had been trying to persuade me to take it, for no other reason than that their rival boatmen had been ridiculing their chances of catching a broadbill out of the big launch. More to please them than for any other reason, I consented to it. How strangely things work out sometimes!

We took the steamer course, and putting the *Gladiator* to nine knots an hour, we headed toward where we had last seen swordfish. When we were well out in the channel I climbed to the crow's nest and began my vigil for the day. The promise of a fine day was indeed stimulating. While scanning the heaving surface of the sea for swordfish fins it was my habit to miss nothing that moved, nor the endless changing waters and colors, nor the aspect of sky or cloud, nor the dim mountains on the mainland.

Many days were barren of life—no fish, no birds, no whales or blackfish—nothing but drab monotony—the gray heaving sea reflecting the fog. Sometimes an east wind blew, cold and raw, whipping up a rough sea. Other days the westerly wind came up early, breaking up the fog banks, changing sky and sea from dull hue to a brilliant blue. Then the little white-crested waves rose and grew and swelled until they were great combers, rolling green and white, with the sunlight shining through. This kind of sea was not good for swordfish, and many were the times we headed back toward the island. Each day was different, somehow, and past experience had taught us that each season had yielded two or three wonderful days. We were always on the lookout for one of these.

Before we were halfway across the channel I believed we had struck one of the great days. But not yet could I be sure. Still, there was a glow on the smooth heaving sea; schools of tuna were breaking white water; the long ripples of sharks showed on the surface; shearwater ducks wheeled and flew like falcons, skimming the water in their swift flight; here and there a sunfish flopped up to fall flatly back; and far in the distance the forked flukes of a whale rose out of the sea, poised and waved and slid down—most majestic sight afforded by the ocean.

When two and a half hours out, and within several miles of the mainland, my roving eye caught sight of two dark sickle-shaped fins cleaving the water half a mile farther on. The old irrepressible thrill went over me.

"Swordfish!" I yelled down to my comrades.

"Where?" they shouted in unison.

"Dead ahead," I replied, and climbed down from the crow's nest.

R. C. and Sid clambered off into the *Little Gladiator*, taking bait and tackle. I followed with cameras. Thad cast us loose and remained on the big boat. The swordfish wove away toward the mainland, and was hard to keep in sight.

"Hurry! Hurry!" I called to Sid. "We'll lose him sure."

Then it seemed that promising day started badly. Sid, with a reputation of being infallible with engines, could not start this one. He spun the wheel and used language equally energetic. But it took fifteen minutes to get the engine started. Meanwhile the swordfish disappeared.

We had endured two months of bad luck, one way or another. I lost patience with Sid and the little boat. We were all downcast. It was impossible to be cheerful. R. C. had nothing to say. I was just as unquenchably determined as he was, only I could not take disaster so serenely. We went back to the *Gladiator*, climbed aboard while the boys tied fast the smaller boat.

No sooner had I reached the crow's nest again when I sighted another broadbill, offshore this time. We ran down on him. I decided against further use of the smaller boat, and we tried to circle him with a bait. When our position was just getting favorable he went down, and did not come up. During the succeeding hour I sighted four more broadbills, two of them over five hundred pounds; and though we acted as swiftly and dexterously as possible, every fish went down before we could get a bait in front of him.

We went on. There was nothing else to do. There were no words wasted on the *Gladiator*. How impossible not to be exasperated and hopeless! Our nerves had been frazzled. I think I took it hardest, yet there was a look on my brother's face that hurt me. My common sense told me that we had exaggerated the importance of catching a broadbill for R. C. What was a fish in the normal lives of men? What fools we were! How we wasted hours, days, weeks, months over these exasperating elusive swordfish! But intelligence and reason in no wise changed the driving passion. It was the pursuit that measured so tremendously. The boy is father to the

R. C.'s First Broadbill, 400 Pounds (Plates lxi to lxiv)
(*The reward of five summers' fishing.*)

PLATE LXI

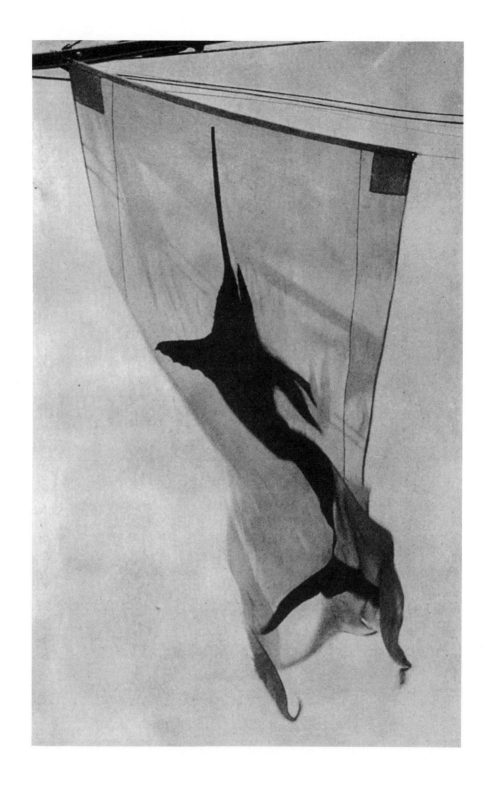

PLATE LXII

PLATE LXIII

PLATE LXIV

man; and R. C. and I had been fishermen since the time when we were able to hold a switch with a thread and a bent pin on the end.

The day turned out to be the most wonderful of sword-fish days—warm, with high diffused fog, and an ocean of smooth heaving, shimmering opal. All objects on the surface were magnified. The air seemed tangible and mysterious. We could not see clearly for a very long distance. Discouraged as I was, I reveled in the beautiful spectral sea, with its loneliness and strangeness. There was a glamour on the water. Gradually I forgot our trials, and the old thrilling hunting instinct returned.

Presently I sighted black dots fully two miles distant, an unusual circumstance, even for the best of eyes. They resembled sea gulls floating on the water. But something about their regular movement and position made me keen to make sure. We headed for them and they turned out to be the fins of a huge broadbill. His dorsal stood two feet out of the water and the lobe of his tail almost as high. The distance between them appeared easily ten feet. Just to see this enormous fish gave me a shock. R. C. said he had a sinking of his stomach.

We tried to work him. Four times we circled him, only to see him sheer away. It was no use. Then we ran down on him and I had a perfect view of him from the crow's nest. He was fifteen feet long, and as big round as a barrel, purple in hue, with a matchless symmetry and grace—a monster birdlike prehistoric kind of creature, incredibly wild and beautiful. Slowly he sank as we neared him. He turned a little on his side, and looked up with big staring black eyes. His four-foot sword was a thing to inspire respect. He did not fear us or the boat any more than he did the water. No one can convince me these swordfish are not dangerous. They ram ships and the swordfishermen's boats on the

Georgian Banks in the Atlantic. They have killed market fishermen. This one slowly sank out of our path, wagging his long slender sword, and faded in the blue water.

"Husky bird, wasn't he?" shouted R. C. from below.

"One thousand pounds!" I called down.

"Huh! Glad he passed me up."

We went on, and soon I sighted another. It was with the strangest sensation that I called to the boys: "Swordfish! Number eight!"

I was possessed by black doubts, yet equally under the dominance of intense hopes. Some time, some day, some one of these wary devils would strike R. C.'s bait. On this occasion I climbed down out of the crow's nest and went back on top of the cabin.

"Hand the rod up to me," I said to R. C. "Maybe I can change your luck."

Without a word he complied, and I stood up and let the barracuda bait out on a long line.

"Sid, keep far away from this fish," I said. He had not been running the boat exactly to suit me. I was hard to please this day. Thad and R. C. stood under me, facing astern, watching operations. I let out more line, until I lost sight of the bait. Keeping fully two hundred feet away from the swordfish, we circled him, and just as we got in favorable position he turned toward the wake of the boat. The bait was a hundred feet beyond the point where he would cross our wake. This position was the right one, very hard to attain.

"Go straight, Sid," I said, and to Thad I called: "Don't slow up!"

Then I wound the big reel to take line in fast. My eyes roved from bait to swordfish. I meant to draw the barracuda even with him when he reached a point thirty or forty feet from the wake. But he flipped his big tail and went down.

"No good!" growled Sid in disgust.

R. C. looked up at me with sharp bright eyes.

"He's going to take it!"

I felt that myself, but I could not voice it. What I should have done was to hand the rod down to R. C. and take up a camera. I did not think of it. Instead I waited in the most quivering suspense. Suddenly the line whipped up. I saw spray fly from it. Then followed a tremendous strike that nearly jerked me overboard. The line whizzed off the reel. I yelled in utter amaze and joy.

"Oh, boy—what a strike! Take the rod—quick!" I shouted in great excitement.

I nearly fell off the deck handing the rod down to R. C. All the time the line was streaking off the reel. R. C. fell into the seat and jammed the rod in the socket.

"Strip off some line! Release the strain," I shouted. I was afraid the swordfish would feel the hook and come up to throw it. That was just what he did, making a splash some distance out.

"Hook him!" I shouted, wildly.

R. C. jerked with all his might and wound the reel frantically. He recovered a lot of line, which told me the swordfish was running toward the boat. I tried to slide down off the deck, facing astern, and was suddenly transfixed there. The water opened with a crack and a crash, not fifty yards away, and out of the white shot up a frightful black enormous fish shape. How incredibly swift! It paralyzed me. The swordfish was huge, yet as quick and limber as a trout. His broad thick back was toward us, and bent like a letter S as he shot up and up, until he was high in the air, fully fifteen feet from the water, the most wondrous and magnificent fish I had ever seen in action.

Crash, he plunged down into the sea! I fell from my perch, and when I got on my feet the broadbill was racing away swifter than any Marlin. Out he leaped again, not so high as before, but with marvelous agility and ferocity. Then he went down again. The line sped off the reel. We looked wildly in all directions. Again the water split white, and out the swordfish leaped straight and clear, his long sharp bill pointed at the sky. He went up high. Then he wagged his huge head. We all saw the barracuda bait swing on the leader six feet above the swordfish. He smashed down and sounded.

Then I dove for my camera, all at once sick over the opportunity I had missed. I had never had such a one before.

"Ah!" breathed R. C., hoarsely.

I wheeled to see that his line had gone slack. R. C. dejectedly reeled in.

"Gone!" I exclaimed, aghast and crushed. That magnificent swordfish had thrown the hook. I had sustained many shocks of disappointment at the loss of swordfish, but this one dwarfed all the others. It was almost too much to bear. R. C. sat motionless, holding the rod, his eyes in the direction where he had last seen the swordfish. All I could do was put a hand on his shoulder. I could not trust my voice then.

"My God! what an awful fish!" ejaculated R. C. in a voice of awe. Then presently he added: "How big was he?"

Thad, old fisherman and sailor, used to disasters of the sea, replied with a calmness inexplicable to me:

"I'd say between five and six hundred."

"Did he jump like that, really, or was I seeing things?" asked R. C.

BROADBILL SWORDFISH LEAPING

PLATE LXV

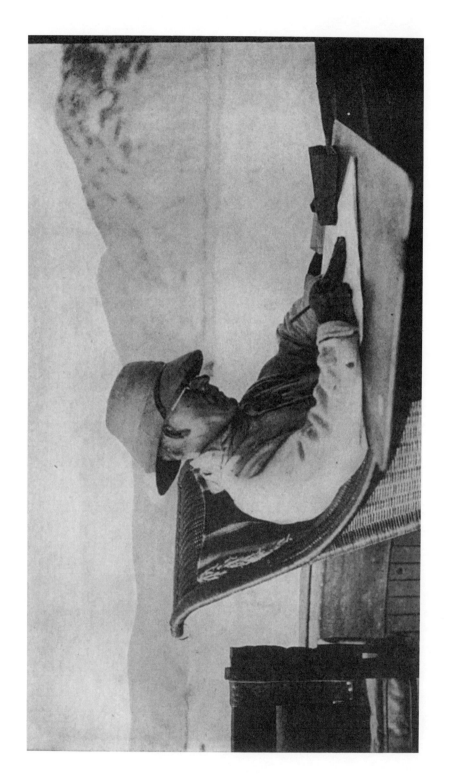

THE AUTHOR

PLATE lxvi.

"He jumped harder, higher, faster than any Marlin we ever saw," I found voice to reply.

We were all silent a moment. No one did anything. The *Gladiator* rolled gently, and the smaller boat bumped against us. R. C. still stared astern.

"I'll never get over that," he said, finally. "Those jumps. Wonderful! Terrible! Unbelievable!"

"Let's see your leader," I said.

We drew it in and all examined it with great curiosity. About half a foot from the hook there was a loop or ring, a complete circle of the fine wire, wound and knotted so tightly I could not pull it loose. It could not have been done better with a pair of pincers.

"What do you know about that!" exclaimed my brother.

"Well, it looks this way to me," I said: "When the swordfish whacked at the bait he missed it and hit the leader. He sure hit it hard, for I had hold of the rod. The force of his blow threw bait and hook clear round his sword. The leader made a loop and knotted and pulled tight. When he felt he was fast to something round his bill he just went wild. He leaped to throw the loop. He sure was a mad fish. Now that hold stayed tight until in his rushes he pointed his sword toward us. Then, of course, you pulled the loop off."

"Ahuh!—What do you suppose would have happened if it had stayed on?" returned R. C.

None of us had any reply for that, but no doubt we all had mental visions of the giant swordfish tearing up the ocean round us, leaping wondrously for our cameras, perhaps imperiling our lives.

"I'll never get over that," was R. C.'s sober final comment.

I have no idea how long we were preoccupied and silent. The *Gladiator* drifted on the opal sea. I was reflecting on the numberless strange sights and adventures I had experienced in my long years of fishing. Always something unexpected and greater could happen. The tigerish leaps of that huge swordfish had been indescribably more wonderful than the leaps of the orca we had photographed in 1922. The orcas leaped prodigiously high, but they were playing. This swordfish was leaping for his life. The leaps were made at the end of long swift runs. He had immense weight and strength. The result—the wildness, grace, beauty, agility, the prodigiousness of those leaps—would forever remain limned on my inner eye—something significant of the life of the ocean.

What else might happen to us that day? Anything might happen. In the nature of events sooner or later would come something that would minify all which had gone before. I might see a whale chased by a swordfish—that rare and extraordinary combat witnessed by so few —a huge eighty-foot cetacean splashing mountains of white water—leaping clear into the air, with the fierce swordfish in the air after him. I had talked with a sailor and a boatman, both of whom had seen such a wonderful thing. I had dreamed of it. Surely I would see it some day. And then—what after that? A sea serpent! For I believe there are sea serpents, and that a few have been seen. A deep-sea fisherman roams the very kingdom of adventure and mystery.

WEIGHING A SWORDFISH ON THE DOCK AT AVALON

PLATE LXVII

VIII

SPACE

SUCH thrilling thoughts did not abide with me when I climbed again to the crow's nest. Reality beset me. I felt like Enos Vera, one of Avalon's best boatmen, when he wailed: "Mos' unluck' day I ever see!" This day had been awful for me—I dared not think how terrible for R. C.—and it was not yet over. To be sure, what made it so tragic was the long fruitless days before. Two months of striving without reward! We were almost distracted, and therefore added to the present misfortune all the weight of the preceding days. It can hardly be explained in words, but I felt it in all my being.

Sid steered the *Gladiator* toward Avalon, and I did not make an objection. It hardly mattered to me what direction we took. Still, from sheer habit I kept a sharp lookout for swordfish fins. When we neared the middle of the channel I espied Danielson's boat, and soon saw that he was flying a kite. Then, about half a mile ahead of us, and the same distance from Danielson, my quick eye caught the dark curved fins of a broadbill.

I looked down at my comrades. Sid was half asleep over the wheel. Thad was polishing one of the big reels. R. C. sat hunched down in the fishing chair—the picture of dejection.

"Swordfish! Number nine!" I boomed.

"Where away?" shouted the alert Thad.

R. C. jerked up and rose out of the seat. "O Lord!" he exclaimed, as if it was impossible to keep down thrilling hopes.

In a moment I was out of the crow's nest, on top of the cabin, to find the boys below all ready. R. C. was standing with his rod, and holding his leader astern. A fresh white barracuda on the hook slipped over the water. From above I directed Sid at the wheel and he called down to Thad below. My orders were to keep far from the swordfish and not to slow down until told. I had not the remotest hope of a strike, but I intended not to overlook any possibilities.

We circled the swordfish and passed in front of him at a good angle, though far away.

"No good!" ejaculated the pessimistic Sid.

"He's about three hundred and fifty pounds, I'd say," said R. C., critically. "Let's try him again."

"Wait!" I called sharply from above. The actions of that swordfish sent a bursting riot of blood all through me. From above I could see him better than the boys below. The barracuda had passed him far away and to this side. But he had turned. He was following it, either by sight or by scent. He was fully seventy-five feet from it when he gave that significant little flip of his great curved tail and went under.

"Say, he's ducked on us!" exclaimed R. C. "Looked like he turned toward that bait."

[170]

R. C. gazed up at me for confirmation, but I did not look at him or say a word. My eyes were piercingly glued to a shadowy purple fish shape getting closer to that barracuda. My hopes choked me. My breast was all tight, my veins on fire! Yet I forced myself to think, to use what judgment I had.

"Thad—slow up!" I called, sharply.

The *Gladiator* slackened. I watched the dim swordfish. He was coming surely. I believed I saw his outline more clearly. Then I called Thad to throw out the clutch. We coasted, glided gently with the momentum of the boat. Swordfish and barracuda were now about twenty-five feet apart. I could see the bait weave and shine, slip through the water.

"Wind a little, R. C.," I called. "Keep your bait moving. Easy. That's enough."

R. C. did as he was bidden. Sid had left the wheel and was standing beside R. C., tense and strung in his excitement. It was easy to see from my brother's attitude that he could not control either wild hopes or miserable doubts.

Gradually the barracuda settled down out of my sight. The long round purple swordfish loomed closer to where the bait drifted—closer, and then made a quick wagging movement.

"*Look out!*" I yelled to R. C. It was a moment fraught with emotions I sternly tried to check. I knew that swordfish would strike. I knew it, yet I could not believe what experience had taught me.

R. C.'s line cracked out of the water, flew up six feet. The shock of the strike was so powerful that both rod and angler jerked forward.

"Wow!" shouted Sid, his sunburnt face suddenly radiant. "He hit it."

I leaped down from the deck, hurriedly found my

camera, and ran to R. C.'s side. He had a queer bright rapt look.

"Sit down," I said. "Get your rod in the socket. . . . I'm sure glad he didn't tangle the leader on that first whack."

"Looks good to me," breathed my brother, wonderingly.

I had a moment of black fear. Suppose R. C.'s bad luck held! It might. The chances were that it would. But I dispelled these swift misgivings. Then the line whipped up again. We were all silent now, waiting and watching. After what seemed an interminable period the swordfish hit the line for the third time. Then an instant after that the line began to slide slowly off the reel. I watched it until fifty feet had steadily slipped off.

"R. C., it's a perfect strike," I said. "He's got the bait and he's not scared. Let him go."

That was a moment of absolute elation for all of us. The line slipped off, gradually faster and faster. R. C. began to finger the reel and square his shoulders. I knew how hard it was for him to wait.

"Let him run," I said, forcefully, hiding my feelings. "You'll hook this bird if you don't bungle it. Give him line."

Half the four hundred yards of line slid off. R. C. began to break under that tense situation. I saw it, but I was adamant.

"Give him a little more."

"But, Doc—I won't have any—left," he panted. Big drops of sweat stood out on his brow. I waited another few seconds. Sid and Thad stood like statues.

"*Now!* Throw on your drag! Jerk and wind with all your might."

Like a demon R. C. swept up and back with the rod,

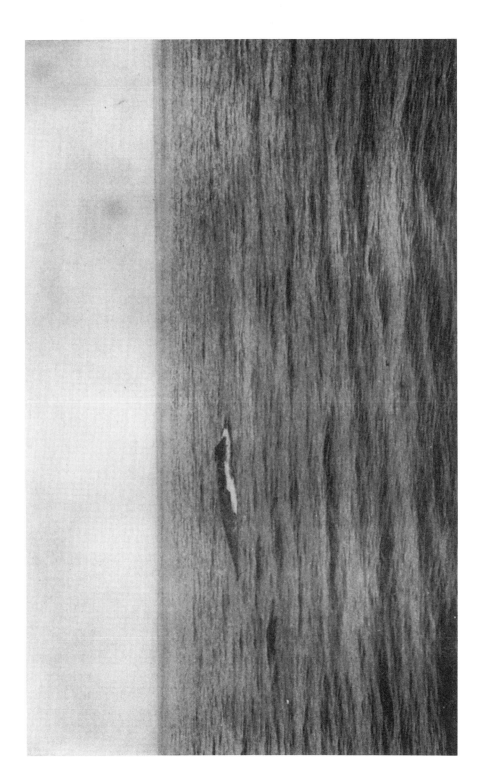

A MONSTER 90-FOOT CALIFORNIA GRAY WHALE

PLATE LXVIII

then lowering it like a flash, he spun the big Coxe reel. Long powerful sweep and wind—again and again— faster and harder he worked.

"Get in that line!" I yelled, brutally. "He's on. Don't give up. Haul in that slack."

Poor R. C. was at the mercy of my drastic orders and his own feelings. Naturally, because the line did not come taut he thought the swordfish had let go. But I knew better. There was something about that line which told me. An experienced fisherman can tell.

"Mr. Grey—he's on yet," interposed Thad, encouragingly.

R. C. kept that swift hard pace, and on the fifteenth sweep of his rod the line came suddenly so tight that it sang like a wire. The rod halted midway in its sweep and bent into a half circle.

"Set the hook!" I shouted.

"Hand it to him!" yelled Sid.

R. C. put shoulders and weight into short tremendous jerks on the bent rod, until I halted him.

"Good! There—you're hooked on!"

This exclamation from me signaled the break in our strain, the moment of let-down. R. C. uttered a queer cry of exultation that had a grim note in it; Sid yelled lustily, like a boy; I pounded R. C. on the back and hilariously bragged of how I had found a swordfish for him and had hooked him on to it; Thad, who had fished for a livelihood since he was five years old, looked at us with amusement, yet on his round face there was a smile of gladness for R. C.

But I soon recovered from that little spell and bethought me of the stern business ahead. Great as it was to hook a broadbill, the conquering of him was the crucial thing. As I straightened up my eye fell upon the *Little Gladiator*, rolling astern of us.

"Thad, pull the little boat close and untie her," I ordered, swiftly. He was as quick as my speech. "Jump in, Sid, and start that engine. . . . Take gaffs—rope!"

Sid almost fell overboard in his eagerness to get into the *Little Gladiator*. He had sponsored the idea of fighting a broadbill out of that little launch.

"What you mean to do?" demanded R. C. Hooked to a swordfish he was a vastly different man, and I feared he might be stubborn.

"Great chance, R. C.," I said, persuasively. "Fight him from the small boat. The sea's calm. I'll go out with you. Thad will follow us."

"But the broadbill—he's pulling!" expostulated R. C.

"Ease the drag. Let him run. But keep the line tight."

"Good night!" uttered R. C. as he stepped on the stern. I reached to steady him, but he did not need any help. Holding the rod up, he jumped down into the little boat, walked back, and sat down in the fishing seat, and jammed the rod in the socket. The change did not take ten seconds, and in that time he was again hauling on the swordfish. With my camera in hand I leaped aboard the *Little Gladiator* and called Thad to cast her loose. He did so and we drifted free.

"Thad, keep close to us, but away from the swordfish. I'll signal to you."

"Aye, aye, sir. I'll be close if he rams you," replied Thad, cheerily. Then he put on the power, and the big boat glided away from us.

At the same instant Sid got the engine of the little boat started and we were off after the swordfish. I was in the bow, where there was a broad seat upon which I laid my open camera. Sid sat on the center seat beside the engine and the steering wheel. R. C. was in the revolving fishing

Z. G. Feeding Bait to Swordfish from Crow's Nest

Plate LXIX

FOUR-HUNDRED-AND-THIRTEEN-POUND BROADBILL

PLATE LXX

chair with his back to me. He was rapidly taking in line.

"All set for a great experience, R. C.," I said, happily. "If he's well hooked—and I think he is—you'll get him, no matter how big he is."

"Lucky this is a smooth sea," observed Sid. "It's the only calm afternoon we've had."

The ocean was smooth and shiny, with great slow heaving swells that lifted the little boat and seemed to carry it along. I felt as if I were afloat on a hollow cork. What a light frail bark it was after riding on the heavy *Gladiator!* There appeared to be something strange and exhilarating in the gentle glide and roll.

"Sure's great!" burst out Sid. "What'd I tell you? Look at me takin' up line!"

Certainly I shared Sid's huge enjoyment, even if I was not as sanguine as he seemed. It was a new and novel experience, and animating it most thrillingly was the glad certainty that R. C. was fighting a broadbill.

"He's coming up," shouted R. C., suddenly.

I followed the direction of the line, and presently saw a smash on the surface about a hundred yards out, and then the big black quivering fins of the swordfish. He lashed the water white. His slender rapier waved like that of a fencer. He rolled and lunged.

"What'll we do?" demanded R. C., anxiously.

"You've got to keep the line tight no matter what he does or how close he gets. That's all. . . . Sid, throw out the clutch. Now, R. C., work on him and let's see what he does."

I stood up in the bow, camera ready, watching the swordfish, hoping he would leap. He threshed away on the surface, taking line from the reel; then he plowed back toward us, making it difficult for R. C. to keep the line taut. Before we realized it he was close, and swiftly the nature of our excitement changed. In that frail boat, scarcely a foot above the surface, with the swordfish churning white water only a hundred feet away, we all answered to natural instincts.

"Let's keep away from him," shouted Sid, hoarsely.

"Sure—out of his way if we can, but we won't run," I replied, grimly.

"Let him come. We got here first," cried R. C. with something of wildness in his voice.

Suddenly I thought of Thad and looked round to find him. The *Gladiator* was not two hundred yards behind us. Thad waved to me and that wave was surely comforting. The presence of our big boat removed the possibility of panic.

"Thad's close, boys," I called, reassuringly. "Let the swordfish ram us! . . . Now, R. C., keep a tight line, but not *too* tight. Sid, be careful not to stall the engine. Try to maneuver as I tell you."

"WHOOP!" pealed out R. C.

I had changed the focus on my camera, and thus lost track of the swordfish for a second. When R. C.'s thrilling yell made me jerk up I was amazed to see the swordfish rushing right at us. It frightened and disconcerted me. I might have taken a wonderful picture of the big fish, dorsal bristlingly erect, huge tail working to and fro, making white swirls and splashes. But I dropped my camera and grasped one of the gaffs.

"Don't gaff him!" yelled R. C. in great excitement.

"Say—I'm not crazy. But if he gets gay I'll biff him on the bean."

My facetiousness was not shared by my comrades. As a matter of fact, I was simply scared silly. No wonder! I had seen swordfish do threatening things, and I had collected much data about their ramming ships and sinking dories and stabbing market fishermen. If I had been

[176]

on the big *Gladiator*, constructed to be safe from possible attack of these monsters, I would have been merely thrilled. But I was in a boat no bigger than the swordfish. He could have smashed it into kindling wood.

I ordered Sid to run, and we crossed in front of the swordfish. I could not watch both the fish and R. C., so I abandoned any idea of keeping an eye on R. C. I forgot him. I did not even see the line. As I was about to heave a breath of relief the swordfish made a circling lunge, splitting the water, shooting spray aloft, and again headed right for us. We were running. I yelled for Sid to turn. The little boat quickly answered her helm. That swift turn saved us—I had no idea from what. Nevertheless, the swordfish, churning the water, bumped our bow hard enough to lift it and send water all over us. His dorsal and tail had slid under the point of our bow. I saw that clearly enough and had a spectacular impression of the fish moving in agitated water. We turned away from him. But he too circled.

"Stop the boat. I can't keep the line tight," yelled R. C.

"He'll ram us," shouted Sid, and it was certain that his face paled.

"Let him ram and be damned!" replied R. C. His red hair was standing erect, his eyes glared, and he looked like a lion. R. C.'s fighting temper had awakened to battle.

"Boys, he's only ranting around," I called. "He didn't charge us. We just got in his way. . . . Wind on him, R. C."

"Soak him—if he comes close—again!" panted R. C.

I did not know whether R. C. meant for me to gaff the swordfish or hit him. And it transpired that the time came quickly when I did not know what I was doing. That swordfish appeared to be everywhere and always near the boat. We could not shake him. While I ran from bow to stern, and back again, brandishing a gaff, I saw that R. C. was working frantically over his rod and that Sid was wildly operating wheel and clutch at the same time. The swordfish got no closer than twenty feet, yet it seemed time and time again he would come right to us. He would go under and then come up. Whenever he disappeared close to us that was an awful moment of suspense. But when he lifted his wild lean head and wagged it, describing a semicircle with his frightful sword—that was the worst. I could hear the sword swish over the surface. Excited and off my balance as I was, I noticed some actions and some features clearly enough to remember well. Once I saw the white foam suddenly redden with blood. This caused me to yell wildly to the boys that he was bleeding—he was disabled—he was our fish.

Whether long or short, that spell of rushing around madly on the surface came to an end and our quarry sounded. For the first time he went deep. Five hundred feet he whizzed off and then he stopped down there in the depths. I was immensely relieved.

"Whew! Were you—guys around—when it happened?" asked R. C., pantingly.

Sid exploded. "My gosh! but the *Gladiator* an' Thad looked good to me!"

I concealed the ravages of my own wild state and assumed a calm and wise air.

"Nice little flurry he gave us," I said. "But it didn't fuss me—much."

"Ha! Ha! Ha!" roared my brother, diabolically. "You acted damn funny."

"How so?" I inquired, feigning surprise.

"You ran round like mad. You fell over Sid and kicked me. You lost your hat overboard. And you

R. C. with 368-pound Swordfish. This Fish Was in Poor Condition.
Note Parasites

Plate lxxi

The "Gladiator" About to Dock, Flying the Swordfish Flag

Plate LXXII

jabbered like an idiot—giving Sid and me orders what to do."

"No engineer or boatman could ever have carried out your orders," added Sid, solemnly.

"Well, I dare say you boys were pretty badly excited," I replied, blandly. "I notice, however, that the sword-fish is still on. I sure had a hard time keeping R. C. to a tight line."

"Tight line!" ejaculated my brother in amaze. "Say, I couldn't keep a tight line. I saw the line loop round his dorsal fin as he swam at us. He had slack line all the time."

"Well, it's tight enough now and I advise you to go to work on him."

With that, R. C. settled down to the laborious task ahead of him, and I took a restful seat. I enjoyed watching him. He had a long, slow, easy, powerful sweep and he had the endurance to keep it up. Never in the early hours of a fight did he rest his rod on the gunwale.

He was using my new heavy tackle, the new reel J. A. Coxe had built for me, and a specially made thirty-nine-thread line, four hundred yards long. In past years we had broken so many twenty-four-thread lines on sword-fish that we had determined to employ lines fairer to the fish and certainly more sportsmanlike for the angler. Innumerable tuna and swordfish are broken off every summer at Catalina, and they die a lingering death or become fodder for sharks. Tackle should be suitable to the size of the game—heavy enough to enable both angler and fish to fight hard. Light tackle for heavy fish is slow, uncertain, brutal. It sacrifices a hundred fish to one that is caught. If men must follow their primitive instinct for fishing they should make it a healthy red-blooded fighting sport.

It was great to see R. C. working on this heavy fish

with proper tackle. In half an hour he had pumped and lifted the swordfish up to a reasonable depth. Manifestly the hook had been well set. Time and labor would surely bring a reward. Sid was elated and babbled like a boy. R. C. sat bareheaded, and the light shone on his face, that wore a slight pleased smile. He did not talk any more and had entered the second phase of his Herculean task. Still, I could feel how splendid and full was this early hour of the fight. Recompense for the five long summers of toil and the many defeats and the swordfish he had lost!

For the next hour and a half there was a sameness and regularity to R. C.'s work that made it monotonous. He was like a machine. He resembled a winch. The time came when he could hold that swordfish, lead him or head him, as we call it, and thus he entered the third stage of the fight.

Strange to say, the wind did not rise—the ever-sure westerly failed that day, and the ocean remained calm. I had nothing to do but watch R. C. and let my eyes rove over the shimmering opal water. The sun was westering, no longer hot. A swordfish showed on the surface, not far from us, and remained up for a long time. He was a small one. I wondered if he was any relation to the big one on R. C.'s line. After a while he wavered away out of sight.

When more than three hours had passed R. C. began to show that he was laboring. He grew slower, weaker. His shirt was wet from sweat. He complained of the harness hurting his back. The water from the line wet his clothes and made a slippery place on the floor. I noted that he no longer held the revolving chair so steadily.

"Shut down on him and let him tow the boat," I suggested.

LONG, SLIM SWORDFISH. A FAST SURFACE FIGHTER

PLATE LXXIII

R. C.'s Smallest Broadbill, 152 Pounds

Plate LXXIV

"Dare we risk it?" he queried.

"Surely. That line won't break."

So we tried it. And it turned out to be a good suggestion. R. C. was careful not to put on too stiff a drag. Sometimes the swordfish pulled out a little line. But in the main he dragged the boat. Sid was in an ecstasy. He raved about the discovery he had made. The swordfish, when first up against the weight of the boat, did not like it at all. He made some rushes, but not swift, and the line paid out readily. Then evidently he wearied of trying to break away from this dragging weight. He slowed down. And he towed the *Little Gladiator* all over the ocean. The big *Gladiator* followed us, growing closer. Thad called cheerily to R. C. The time arrived when the swordfish swam so slowly that the boat barely moved. R. C. recovered his breath and his strength, and several times turned eagerly to work again. But I made him desist.

"Say, that swordfish's licked," complained Sid, impatiently.

"I can pull his head off," declared R. C.

"Wait a little," I said, as I bent over the gunwale and watched the almost imperceptible ripple that proved the boat was moving. At length I turned to R. C.: "Listen. He's darn tired, if he's not licked. Now go at him for all you've got. Hard, slow, steady!"

R. C. swept into action. What he had done before was nothing compared with this.

"Just one more word. Take shorter lifts, so you won't break the rod," I cautioned.

It did appear that R. C. was making good his brag. He hauled the swordfish up and up until only fifty feet of the line was left in the water. Then that swordfish awoke to desperate resistance. The big fight was on and if R. C. lasted the finish was in sight. And it was a strange fight, for the swordfish would wag and jerk ten yards off the reel then slow up so that R. C. got it back. This convinced me our quarry had not been playing 'possum. Otherwise he would have rushed off on a long run.

I stood beside R. C., keeping a keen eye on his every movement. We were nearing the climax. My breast was all clogged with suppressed emotions. I forced a clear head. I restrained my growing wild exultation. Nothing spectacular in the fight now! It was give and take. Yet R. C.'s work now was truly Herculean. His breathing labored to short whistling pants; his arms cracked; the sweat flooded his face. I was worried at the white circles under his eyes—a sign of overexertion and distress in him.

"Better let him tow the boat once more," I suggested, reluctantly, forced to this issue.

"No! How long—have I—been?" he whispered, hoarsely.

"Four hours and ten minutes."

"I've got—something left," added R. C. "Better use it—now—hadn't I?"

I hesitated. All this responsibility was terribly poignant for me. How passionately I wanted R. C. to catch that swordfish! It was as if we were little boys, back in old Zanesville, on the brook where we learned and loved to fish. That thought settled my decision and inflamed me. Swiftly I put on gloves and lifted a gaff over the gunwale.

"*Bring him up!*" I called, and my voice seemed strange in my ears.

R. C. drew a long deep breath and heaved into action. I did not look up at him as I bent over the gunwale, with fascinated gaze on that line. I heard the hum of the stretched line, the rasp of the reel. I heard R. C.'s bones

Z. G.'s Smallest Broadbill, 192 Pounds

Plate LXXV

FOUR HUNDRED AND FIFTY POUNDS

PLATE LXXVI

crack. Not inch by inch, but foot by foot the line came up!

"Boy, you've got him coming," I cried, almost beside myself. "Keep it up—exactly the same. . . . *Oh! I see the leader!*"

As if he had been a steam windlass, R. C. brought that leader up and up, until I bent to the water's edge and grasped it with both gloved hands.

"Stop! I got it!" I yelled.

Sid leaned over to help me, grasping at my hands.

"No! You'll break him off—tear out the hook. . . . Let me— Maybe I can hold him."

"Care—ful," gasped R. C. as if strangled. I felt him place a hand at my belt.

Guardedly I pulled on the leader. Then I got the feel of an immense live fish. At the same instant, fifteen feet down in the clear water, I saw the white-and-purple swordfish swimming on his side. What sensations I experienced! With all the savage frenzy to hold and to kill I yet saw with intense vividness the beauty, wildness, the strange birdlike shape of that swordfish. And so fixed in my mind and will, all through this battle was the idea to avoid blunders, to think swiftly and rightly, that even on the supreme moment I did not pull too hard. I could lift him inch by inch. He sailed to and fro under me, like a beautiful bright shield. He rolled and wearily wove back and forth. His great black forked tail could just wag and that was all. I held the leader tightly, but not so tightly that it could not slip through my hands. Thus I gained and lost. All the time I watched him, saw him in every move and sharp-cut outline. Once I thought—what if I break him off—and my heart swelled in my throat. Emotion and instinct mounted in me until the latter gained the ascendency. After that all was luck.

I lifted on the leader. The great live moving weight

[183]

yielded—more and more. He was coming up. Never in my life had I felt as then. What a frightful, crowded, glorious moment! Still on his side, he swam out from under me—out and upward—his long fierce sword cleaving the water. Then he pulled the leader out of my hands.

"I—couldn't hold—him!" I gasped, as I straightened up.

"Doc, he's my meat," declared R. C. "See—I can hold him." My brother's face was purple except for the white shadows under his eyes. Victory, like a beacon light, shone there.

"He's licked!" yelled Sid, hilariously. "He's turned over—he's floatin' up!"

Indeed, it did seem true. I could see, though I could not move. R. C. had let go six or eight feet of line, and that with the length of leader put the swordfish some twenty-odd feet from the boat. As he sheered up to the surface his black sharp bill stuck out. He rolled on his side, his tail just moving. What exquisite coloring of purple, bronze, and silver! I was actually paralyzed at the sight of the strange sea monster, his black eyes watching us. In them I seemed to see the spirit to slay if his strength had not been spent.

He rolled again and both dorsal and tail came out. The movement brought him closer to the bow. Sid leaped over the engine seat and grasping the leader, that came up near the bow, he began to haul.

"Easy! Easy!" I found voice to utter.

Sid was all pale, strained and tense, but he did not bungle it. I threw a gaff to him, and looked for the other. It was already in the bow, leaning on the gunwale. R. C. stood up out of the seat and threw off his drag. That action signified certainty. Sid hauled cautiously. The swordfish sheered round the bow, to the other side. His mouth gaped. He wagged wearily as Sid drew him closer.

"Doc—it's all over—but the fireworks," said R. C.

Sid held the leader in his left hand, and grasping the gaff, with a swift sure move he extended it out over the water. This was the last crucial instant. I wanted to yell another caution, but my voice was gone. Sid waited. The great swordfish rolled over and paralleled the boat. Then with slow careful lunge Sid gaffed him.

I expected a tremendous roar of exploding water and a deluge on board, as had been my experience before. But R. C.'s broadbill gave the boat a sounding whack with his tail, and lay quiet.

"Rope that tail," called R. C., sharply.

I picked up the rope, opened the noose, and bending over I passed it under the widespread, gently wagging tail, and sprang up with an Indian whoop of joy. R. C. looked queer, like a sick boy, yet glad over something, and he suddenly sat down. Thad turned loose the siren whistle on the *Gladiator*.

That day, near sunset, a thousand spectators saw the swordfish weighed in on the pleasure pier—an even 400 pounds! R. C. had caught his broadbill!

IX

HEAVY TACKLE FOR HEAVY FISH

AFTER years of trial and experience I came to the conclusion that the standard twenty-four-thread line was not heavy enough for broadbill swordfish, not to mention big tuna. What a familiar story— the hooking of a broadbill and wearing out of the line! I have recorded hundreds of cases in my notebooks. The Medway Club of Nova Scotia, and other Eastern fishing clubs, allow thirty-nine-thread lines for heavy fish. Summer after summer R. C. and I kept on breaking twenty-four-thread lines on swordfish. Last season, 1923, we decided to use tackle which we were convinced was more sportsmanlike for the angler and fairer to the swordfish.

I had constructed for me the famous Coxe reel, much larger than the 9 o, and it cost fifteen hundred dollars. I had special lines made, thirty-nine-thread, four hundred yards long. These were to be used on broadbills alone. For tuna we used the regular Coxe 9 o reels, and especially made twenty-four-thread lines, with a breaking strain of eighty-five pounds when wet. We tried a thirty-nine-thread line on tuna, but found that its use was impractical, because the line when wet was too heavy for the kite. We frankly exhibited this tackle to boatmen and anglers alike. Most of the boatmen, at least, appeared favorably impressed, and wished they had something of the same kind to use.

On June 1st we started out in the *Gladiator*, fresh, eager, determined, with as many thrills as if it was our first venture for big game of the sea. For ninety-odd days the *Gladiator* went out, missing only one day—the Fourth of July. What that means only few anglers can appreciate. As a reward we had the greatest fishing experience of our lives.

We caught forty tuna, most of which weighed over 100 pounds. R. C. had the largest of that season at Avalon—146½ pounds, also one of 140. On June 29th we took six large tuna: 110, 114, 115, 118, 118, 130 pounds. All these tuna, the most of which R. C. caught, were taken on the Coxe reels, and the special twenty-four-thread lines. R. C. broke one line and I broke a leader.

That very day most of the boatmen reported breaking lines on tuna. Tad Gray lost three, and according to Boerstler's report another boatman broke off six. I saw Smith Warren hook a number of tuna from the schools we were working. That night he did not bring in a fish. I said to him: "Where's your fish? Every time I looked at your boat you were hooked on." He threw up his hands in disgust, and that meant nothing but broken lines. These boatmen all had anglers using an inferior grade of twenty-four-thread lines, with breaking strain limited to sixty pounds. These lines cost from eight to twelve dollars, according to length. Mine were five hundred yards long and cost thirty dollars each.

A tuna breaking off with big hook in throat or mouth,

dragging leader and line, will not live long. Huge sharks follow the schools of tuna. Once these monsters scent blood they are veritable tigers. So that June 29th there must have been at least a ton of tuna meat gone to the maws of the sharks. To break off tuna after tuna on inadequate lines is hardly a sportsmanlike procedure. Even if it were, the interest of conservation should prohibit an angler from doing it.

We used our great Coxe reels and the wonderful thirty-nine-thread lines on broadbill swordfish. We had an exceedingly thrilling and memorable experience, which I shall write of fully at another time.

R. C. caught his first broadbill, for which he has been laboring for five years—a 400-pound swordfish, taken in four hours and twenty minutes, after a spectacular fight. How he did pull on that big fish! I was afraid he might break the Murphy hickory rod, but not the reel or line. He said afterward that he had never had such a feeling of security as this tackle gave him.

On August 21st I caught a broadbill, 262 pounds, in four and one-half hours. The next day I caught another, 298 pounds, in two hours and a quarter. And on August 31st I took my third broadbill of the season, 360 pounds, in two hours and forty minutes.

That ended our broadbill season. We had sighted 140 swordfish, worked 94—and by worked I mean we got a bait in front of that number; we had 11 strikes, hooked 7 fish, and caught 4.

September 1st, which was our last day, we devoted to trying for a Marlin swordfish. And R. C. had the staggering good fortune to add to his already wonderful list of Marlin. He caught a 324-pound fish—one hour and forty-five minutes. He has now five great Marlin to his credit: 300, 304, 328, 354, 324. There is no other angler who has caught more than one 300-pound fish and indeed few who have caught one. R. C.'s 354-pound Marlin was the largest ever recorded.

His 324-pound Marlin was a most beautiful specimen. Upward of ten thousand visitors to Avalon, a holiday crowd, went out on the dock to look at this fish. To see them, and hear a few of their comments, was something to remember.

Before we left Avalon several boatmen asked me for one of the thirty-nine-thread lines. Then, the last day, Harry Adams called upon me and amazed me by wanting to buy one of my thirty-nine-thread lines. Adams is conceded by the Tuna Club to be their greatest angler.

Adams told me of two fights he had recently had with broadbills, the second of which lasted seven hours and fifteen minutes. Both swordfish wore out the twenty-four-thread lines.

"It makes me sick to go out there, hook a big fish, and lose him because my line wears out," said Adams to me. "I'm not going to do it any longer. These twenty-four-thread lines are not strong enough for swordfish over three hundred pounds. I think you are years ahead of all of us. Now I want you to sell me one of your thirty-nine-thread lines. I'll use it, and when I catch a broadbill I will call a meeting of the directors of the Tuna Club and tell them flatly that you are right and they are wrong. If they want to make a new rule fair to anglers and to the broadbill, well and good. But I'm going to use a thirty-nine-thread, anyhow."

I presented Adams with one of my new thirty-nine-thread lines and I surely hoped he would catch a 500-pounder on it. This statement of his made a singularly happy climax to our wonderful fishing season. Adams is a great angler, and what is more a fine, stalwart, splendid type of Westerner, a man whose integrity would never be questioned by anyone. He was upholding my judgment at a critical time. Some day all broadbill anglers will conform to this heavier tackle.

My published conclusions, that resulted from long experience with heavy fish and sprang from my deepest conviction, have brought a storm down upon my head.

It seems I had thrown a monkey wrench into the works of the light-tackle advocates. Letters were published, some of them written and signed by fishermen earnest and honest enough, but who had not my experience at the game and who, moreover, were obsessed with the attractiveness of light tackle without having realized its limitations.

Before I had taken to heavy tackle on heavy fish, I had for twelve years used light tackle. Indeed, I introduced it at Long Key for sailfish. But I cannot see light tackle, that is to say, a nine-thread line and six-ounce rod, for swordfish and tuna. Elsewhere, more than once, I have told why. The advocates of light tackle, rather few in number at that, claim it is more sportsmanlike to catch a big fish on a delicate rig.

That sounds all right. It sounds fine, but it is deceptive to the inexperienced angler and the layman. How about the ten-to-one ratio of heavy fish that break the light tackle and swim away with hooks in their throats? The light-tackle men dodge this question or deny it. They seldom or never report any broken lines. But I *know*. And I have always felt it my duty, unpleasant as the result may be, to tell the *truth* as I see it.

Anonymous letters, wholly abusive, and vile in some instances, were published and circulated to discredit and defame me. The writer of any anonymous letter proclaims his status to the world. I did not care to know who wrote them, but my friends in the Tuna Club were not backward about informing me.

THIS WAS AN OLD WARRIOR, 515 POUNDS IN WEIGHT. NOTE THE SCARS
RECEIVED IN BATTLES WITH OTHER SWORDFISH

PLATE LXXVII

This period was rather a hard one for R. C. and me to stick out. Every time we caught a fish we heard that it had been harpooned, or shot, or lassoed, or caught any way except fairly.

Some things, however, are hard to overlook. For instance, as already related, after five years of persistence and defeat my brother R. C. caught his first broadbill. No one could have guessed what that meant to us. While he was fighting this fish a boatman with his angler happened by, and hove to and watched the battle for half an hour. That night it was reported in the Tuna Club that I had been seen fighting my brother's fish. It might amuse my detractors, surely surprise them, to learn that remark went all over the world. But they knew that neither horses nor men could have pulled that rod from R. C.'s hands.

This is another illustration of the only drawback to the great sport of big-game sea fishing.

X

THE DEADLY AIRPLANE-WIRE LEADER

IN the Log of the *Gladiator*, there is mention of the airplane-wire leader. It is necessary to give the said leader more space in this volume, so that its use and nature will be clearly understood. Airplane-wire leader means nothing to the layman, and next to nothing to five million or more American anglers.

Years ago we used to make tarpon and tuna and swordfish leaders out of stiff piano wire. A leader, I should perhaps explain, is the six or ten or fifteen feet of wire, upon one end of which is the hook, and the other the fishing line. If wire were not used, fish with sharp teeth and fins would soon cut off.

Three years ago a newcomer to Catalina introduced a new leader in Avalon fishing. It was quite a mystery for weeks. I never saw a piece of this wire until a boat-man showed it to me in strict secrecy. It appeared to be a bright thin pliable twisted wire.

It did not interest me particularly. But when two broadbill swordfish were caught in quick succession, and

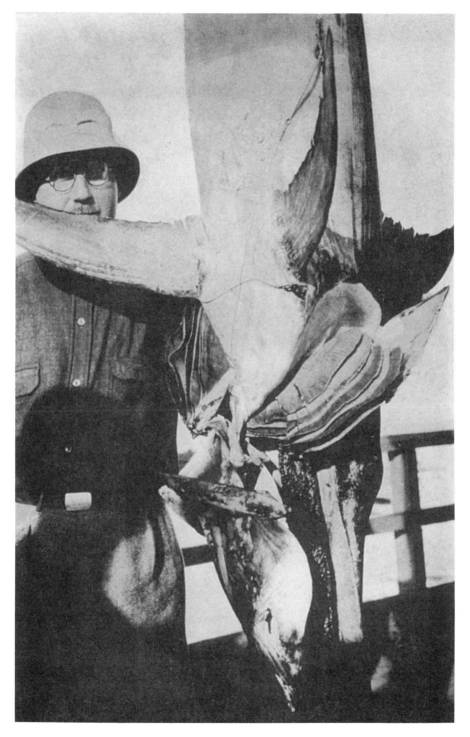

MR. MARTIN WITH SWORDFISH CAUGHT IN SIX MINUTES

PLATE LXXVIII

in extraordinarily short time, I grew curious. I saw the second swordfish, which was cut to pieces. The first one had been hauled aboard in a very few minutes. The boatman then told me that this swordfish had strangled in the airplane-wire leader and had come up dead.

After that we began to hear more about this leader, though we were fully three years in learning the method used. During those years a number of swordfish, including three world-record broadbills, were caught in succession, one for each year, weighing respectively 474 pounds, 528 pounds, and 571 pounds. The anglers who caught the last two named were comparatively new to Catalina waters, and had never been known to fish for broadbills. These anglers took particular pains to specify the remarkably short time in which they had caught their fish.

If they had been old hands at the broadbill game, or had any love or appreciation for this grandest of game fish, or had even understood the strenuous toil a few of us had undergone to catch a broadbill, I think they would have been a little shy about mentioning the brevity of time. But the point they wished to make—which was to emphasize the record short time for landing these fish— was the weak thing about it. Phenomenal luck or extraordinary skill and strength might have accounted for it. As it turned out it was neither.

The airplane wire is very thin and strong, and as pliable as a cord. In fact it cannot be kept straight. It loops like a lasso, in or out of the water. If you hold a six-foot length in one hand and strike it with the other it will fly all around your arm and bind quick as a flash. If you pull on it you make the tangle worse. The harder you pull the tighter the wire binds. It never slips or lets go. It has to be unwound.

Now a broadbill swordfish has a long sword, and a

great notched tail. He always hits his food with his sword. When he hit a bait on one of those airplane leaders, if it was slack, the leader flew around the sword; and when the fish rolled and surged he would soon become entangled. Then when the leader was pulled tight the fish was either cut to pieces—for this wire cuts like a blade—or strangled, or rendered helpless.

And there you are. This new method of angling was simply, when feeding a bait to a swordfish, to slack off a lot of line, and let it hang loose. If the swordfish struck, the chances were a hundred to one he would get tangled. And if he was tangled he might as well have been lassoed.

My brother and I tried out this method until we proved it, and that was enough for us. Captain Mitchell also used this new kind of wire, but not in the manner described. We strike our swordfish on a tight line, and in almost all cases we have a long hard battle on our hands.

Moreover, there is a more serious drawback about this airplane-wire leader than its unsportsmanlike use in regard to fish. It is a most deadly and treacherous instrument. It should be used with extreme caution. We narrowly escaped injury several times while trying it out. Of course the danger is negligible so long as you do not have a fish on or while you are fighting one. It is when you get the fish up to the boat that danger threatens. For this reason I never allowed the boatman to gaff a fish until it was completely spent.

Say, for instance, the boatman takes the leader in his hands and hauls the fish close. Six, or eight, or ten feet of that infernal leader coils and loops and springs behind the boatman, in the cockpit, or at least in front of him. Suppose the fish gives a tremendous lunge and tears the leader from the boatman's hands. This happens even with experienced boatmen. One of those flying loops of

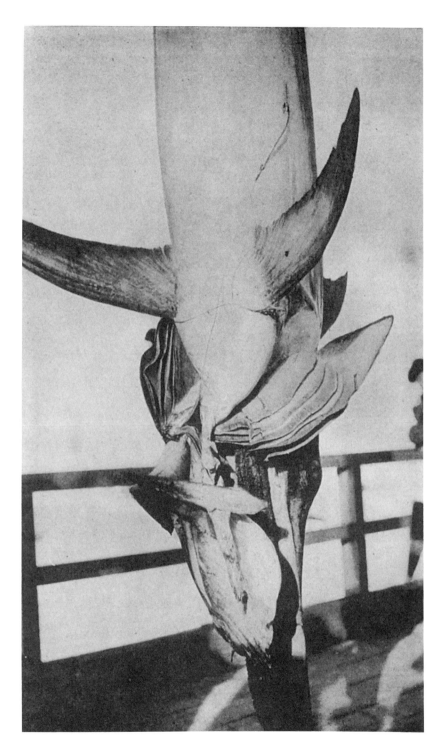

THE DEADLY AIRPLANE-WIRE LEADER (Plates lxxix to lxxxii)
(*Note where the hook catches and how the wire tangles. Note particularly swordfish
with head nearly severed. This fish was caught in six minutes!*)
PLATE LXXIX

PLATE LXXX

PLATE LXXXI

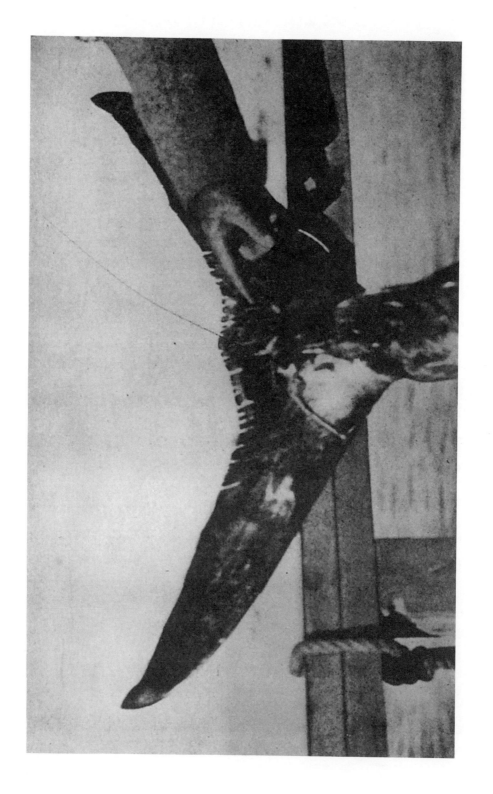

PLATE LXXXII

wire might catch his hand or coil round his neck. In the latter case it would mean decapitation. It could happen very easily.

Mr. Martin, who introduced this leader to Catalina waters, lost part of the fingers of his hand in precisely this manner. If he did not before realize the deadly nature of this leader he surely does now. And I know he has developed into too fine a fisherman and sportsman to be any longer proud of his catching a broadbill in six minutes! There has never been so destructive an article of fishing tackle invented as this same wire leader. And to my knowledge there has never been one so unsportsmanlike, when used as I have described. It does away with the fight. Anyone can catch a broadbill on an airplane-wire leader, if he or she will fish long enough to get one tangled.

Its use at Catalina has almost killed the grand sport of swordfishing, and brought into casual note the most magnificent fighting fish of the seven seas.

XI

LOREN GREY'S FIRST FISH STORY

MY BOY Loren, aged ten, is not merely a chip of the old block—he is a whole chunk. He elected himself as bait catcher for the Z. G. outfit, and the barracuda he is holding up in the photograph was actually the bait I used in the capture of my world-record broadbill—582 pounds.

Loren was as proud of catching the bait as I was of catching the great swordfish. I told him that it was high time he wrote his first fish story, and here it follows:

THE BARRACUDA, THE WOLF OF THE PACIFIC AND FISHING IN CATALINA ISL.

by

LOREN GREY

Last summer, 1926, we decided to go fishing around the northeastern part of the island. Romer, Johnney, and myself were the members of the party and we decided to go on June 28, 1926. The day set to go fishing dawned with a heavy fog on the sky, but it soon gave way to clouds. We started out early so as to be there before the clouds cleared away. When we got about 3 miles from the bay of Avalon we put out a teaser and our trolling lines and trolled around the little cove where we were in.

As I was watching the sea I saw a large black body rise out of the water and go down again to send up a stream of water 30 feet high, and then a broad black tail showed for an instant and then went down to show again a few feet nearer.

Suddenly I had a strike that nearly jerked the rod from my grasp as the line zipped out and I found myself hooked on to a fast fish. He was very fast but not very specticculer. After a 15 minute fight I pulled in 6½ pounds of barracuda. We caught no more fish that day.

The barracuda is the wolf of the sea, for it has teeth from 1/16 of an inch to 1 inch long. Its back is a dark gray with a white stomach. It ranges from 2 to 12 feet in length and from 3 to 400 pounds in weight.

1926, AND THE WORLD-RECORD BROADBILL

The Log of the *Gladiator* will show how R. C. and I roamed the seas and wore out our boatmen along with ourselves, but it scarcely does justice to our unremitting efforts to think of and evolve things to improve the game of swordfishing.

Several times we made improvements on the *Gladiator*, and in the winter of this year, 1926, we put in a new mast, raised the crow's nest ten feet higher, and included in it a fishing chair with rod-socket, so that we could hook and fight broadbills from that advantageous height.

We had been years perfecting the *Gladiator*, the special Coxe reels and Swastika lines and Pflueger swordfish hooks, and lastly our method of fishing. No time or labor or study or expense had been spared.

At the beginning of the 1926 season I believed that we were going to have a wonderful climax to all our swordfishing. I had learned something in New Zealand, and felt that we would profit by that. And as it turned out we had more wonderful luck than even I had dreamed and hoped.

The Log of the *Gladiator* records ten broadbill swordfish, five for R. C. and five for me, including the world-record 582 pounds, and another over 500, all caught in Catalina waters, within fifteen miles of Avalon.

There is no doubt that our great success was mainly due to the following several details: We kept everlastingly at it. We could locate more fish than a dozen ordinary boats. Not only was the crow's nest wonderful for sighting broadbill fins, but it was more than that as a place to work from. We kept far away from swordfish, so that they were not aware of the boat. We could see every move they made. We could let out 200 yards of line and still see the bait, and place it right in front of a swordfish. See him hit it! I can conceive of little more thrilling in the fishing line, or on a fishing line, either!

Not the least of our pleasure in our success was to run back to Avalon with the red flag flying at the masthead, to blow a clarion blast from the *Gladiator* whistle, and to see the pier fill with excited spectators. Sometimes thousands of summer visitors massed at the end of the pier to see the swordfish weighed and photographed. On these occasions R. C. or I would have to stand the battery of hundreds of cameras and shake hands until we broke away from the pier.

Naturally our brimming cup of 1926 angling joy and reward was embittered by several caustic and biting drops, only one of which do I care to publish.

We took out another well-known English sportsman —Mr. C. Alma Baker. The day was fine. I sighted a swordfish and had the luck to have him strike and get hooked, as I told fully in the Log. As soon as it was possible I handed the rod down from the crow's nest and followed.

We put Mr. Baker on the rod. Now out of deference to him, I had used the Alma rod and reel, both designed by Mr. Baker, and built by Hardy Bros. of England. He appeared to have more interest in the tackle than in the plunging swordfish at the end of the line. This was well enough, and amused us, while Mr. Broadbill kept far away from the boat and deep down. But when in a half hour or more he came up and charged us on a slack line it began to be serious, with at least imminent danger of losing the fish. Mr. Baker had never fought a broadbill and was at a loss to know what to do when the fish kept weaving and crossing our stern, sometimes going under us, while we were trying to keep away from him. In the end I had to take the rod from Mr. Baker; and I had a pretty hard time myself keeping clear of the propeller and pulling the leader to Sid's hands.

All this time Captain Mitchell had watched us from his boat, which he kept at a distance of several hundred yards. He told us afterward that there had been two broadbills, one of which he was working when we came up. He and his son and a guest had watched all the fight.

This broadbill was a small one, as broadbills go, but he counted; and I was particularly happy to have had Mr. Baker know what such a fish felt like on a line, and to see one plow round the boat in plain sight. Mr. Baker was immensely delighted with the working of the Hardy tackle.

That night my son Romer came home early, in high

dudgeon, to announce that it was all over town that we had been seen to shoot the swordfish. I had nothing to say, but I threw up my hands and decided I had best stay home. But R. C. and Captain Mitchell went downtown and found that Romer had not exaggerated. They traced the statement to the pier and the boatmen, and finally pinned it down to an angler who had often defamed us.

Upon hearing their report I said: "It seems to me this angler has picked out the wrong day to accuse us of shooting swordfish."

"By Jove! it's most absurd!" exclaimed the practical Captain Mitchell. "Don't these anglers know that it's impossible to get a swordfish if it's shot? That was tried out by the market fishermen on the Nova Scotia banks. A swordfish sinks like lead."

When Mr. Baker heard that he had been made a party to the shooting of a swordfish—well, I found out what an angry Englishman is like. He had some pertinent things to say.

Captain Mitchell wrote to the man who had started the story, pointedly and in a sportsmanlike manner, and gave him opportunity to explain such a preposterous assertion, and to apologize for what might have been a hasty and ill-tempered remark. But he never answered the letter.

A few days later an acquaintance of mine, while dining at the Lions' Club in Los Angeles, heard another angler speak out brazenly before a dozen men: "Sure Grey shoots his swordfish!"

And so the poison spreads.

At the conclusion of this volume, which I have been ten years in writing, I apologize to my friends, some of whom belong to the Tuna Club, and to the hundreds of thousands of readers who do me honor, for having mentioned a few of the unpleasant obstacles I have encoun-

LOREN GREY, THE BAIT CATCHER

PLATE LXXXIII

The Fins of the World's Record Swordfish Just Before Striking. This Is the Greatest and Most Thrilling Sight to a Sea Angler

Plate LXXXIV

HOOKED ON

PLATE LXXXV

R. C. Congratulating Z. G.

Plate lxxxvi

tered in my long labors to collect the material for a sword-fish and tuna book.

Now as to the 582-pound world-record broadbill which I was so long in catching and which fulfilled an ambition relentlessly cherished, I can only say that the event of capture was as great as the fish.

I have thought about it so much, and felt so deeply over it, that a long story of my impressions and emotions and labors on this fish would perhaps seem to many readers as somewhat too poignant writing. Always I had intended to try to write the most wonderful story about the capture of my world-record broadbill when that happy day came. But it came, and I cannot write as I would.

Let it suffice for me to make some simple statements.

I sighted this great broadbill at a long distance. When we approached close enough for working, his fins were just tipping the rippling blue water. He seemed to have length, but we could not tell anything about his bulk.

There was nothing spectacular in his strike, but when I came up hard on him I felt a tremendous weight. He did not leap or thresh on the surface. He sounded and gave me all I could do to keep him from taking all the six hundred yards of line. Never had the *Gladiator* been maneuvered so well and skillfully as on that memorable day.

I was fresh from long weeks of strenuous fishing in New Zealand. My hands were hard, my arms and back inured to the dragging weight of heavy fish. I had been in training, so it seemed, for this battle. I had the endurance and I had the tackle.

Farnsworth, the famous Avalon boatman, and his angler, Mr. Thomas, circled round us for an hour, watching me fight that fish. It was a compliment. I believe they were interested to see that heavy Shaver dualwood rod bend like a buggy whip.

I fought and beat this broadbill in five hours and a half. There is no doubt that but for my New Zealand training I would have given out on this swordfish and have been whipped, as I had been so often before. But as it happened, I was fit, the boatmen keen and resourceful and tireless—they must have thrown that heavy clutch in and out a thousand times—R. C. the most inspiring and helpful of comrades, and the sea not rough.

When at last I brought him up from his last thousand-foot level I knew I had the record. He was still alive, but spent, and gave no trouble when gaffed. He floated away a little from the side of the boat, while Sid and Thad slacked on the rope they had noosed over his tail. And then I could stand pantingly, to gaze at his stupendous size and appalling beauty. He was purple in color, smooth as silk, without the blemishes and ugly scars and parasites common to swordfish, immensely round like the body of a horse, symmetrical and graceful, expressive of speed and strength and wildness beyond words to describe. He looked to be fifteen feet in length, but it turned out he was an inch or so over thirteen.

We broke the block and tackle in our first effort to load him, and had to repair and strengthen it before we got him on board. While the *Gladiator* raced homeward over a purple sunset sea I sat on deck, gazing at my prize and then aloft at the streaming white flag with its red swordfish. After ten years of fishing for this swordfish, that surely was a ride.

Amid thousands of excited clamoring onlookers we weighed him in, while breathlessly we guessed at his weight. R. C. came closest with 600 pounds. I had guessed 700. Sid refused to guess, and I hazarded a greater number. But he weighed 582, and that was enough for me.

Then they left him hanging there for the edification of the crowds. I gazed long up at this magnificent fish creature that I had slain, and for once I suffered no remorse. Ten years! With all they meant! I might, indeed, no doubt, would some day catch a larger sword-fish, but there would be a vast difference.

I had him mounted by Mrs. Parker, widow of the famous Avalon taxidermist, and I sent him to be placed in my collection of fishes in the Museum of Natural History, New York City. Perhaps in years to come I will go there and look at him, to recall in wonder what I went through to capture him. And I will recall what I have often said and written—to catch a fish is not all of fishing.

THE END